D0246646

This Book belongs to the Library of King Edward VI's Grammar School, Guildford, Surrey

SUN AND SOLAR SYSTEM

How to use this book

Welcome to *Space Science*. All the books in this set are organized to help you through the multitude of pictures and facts that make this subject so interesting. There is also a master glossary for the set on pages 58–64 and an index on pages 65–72.

The text is organized into chapters.

Capitals show key glossary terms. They are defined in the quick reference glossary.

Quick reference glossary. All these glossary entries, sometimes with further explanation, appear in the master glossary for the set on pages 58–64.

Chapter heading.

Photographs and diagrams have been carefully selected and annotated for clarity. Captions provide more facts.

Links to related information in other titles in the *Space Science* set.

Atlantic Europe Publishing

First published in 2004 by
Atlantic Europe Publishing Company Ltd.

Copyright © 2004
Atlantic Europe Publishing Company Ltd.
First reprint 2004

Author
Brian Knapp, BSc, PhD

Art Director
Duncan McCrae, BSc

Senior Designer
Adele Humphries, BA, PGCE

Editors
Mary Sanders, BSc, and Gillian Gatehouse

Illustrations on behalf of Earthscape Editions
David Woodroffe and David Hardy

Design and production
EARTHSCAPE EDITIONS

Print
WKT Company Limited, China

This product is manufactured from sustainable managed forests. For every tree cut down, at least one more is planted.

Space science – **Volume 2: Sun and solar system**
A CIP record for this book is available from the British Library

ISBN 1 86214 364 1

Picture credits
All photographs and diagrams NASA except the following:
(c=center t=top b=bottom l=left r=right)

Earthscape Editions 3, 6, 7b, 11t, 18–19, 28t, 30–31, 39, 40, 47, 48–49, 52; *Jim Klemaszewski, Arizona State University/NASA* 54–55; *courtesy Dr. Alexander Kosovichev/Stanford University, European Space Agency, and NASA* 32; *Royal Swedish Academy of Sciences* 26–27, 29t; *courtesy of SOHO consortium (SOHO is a project of international cooperation between ESA and NASA)* front cover, 12, 13bl, 13br, 14, 15 (*and inset*), 16–17, 20-21, 24–25, 29b, 34, 35, 36–37, 42–43, 44–45.

The front cover shows the Sun; the back cover, the solar system.

NASA, the U.S. National Aeronautics and Space Administration, was founded in 1958 for aeronautical and space exploration. It operates several installations around the country and has its headquarters in Washington, D.C.

CONTENTS

▲ The surface of the Sun.

1: INTRODUCTION

The Sun is a **STAR** that lies at the center of the solar system—that is, our star's system. The solar system is made up of the Sun and a collection of bodies that **ORBIT** around it, such as the nine **PLANETS** and their **MOONS**, **COMETS**, and **ASTEROIDS**.

The first part of this book deals with the Sun, and its position in **SPACE**. The relationship of the Sun to its planets and the rest of the solar system is dealt with in more detail on pages 46 to 57.

Getting a cosmic perspective

The Sun contains over 99% of the entire **MASS** of the solar system. In space terms, therefore, the Sun is the only significant body in our part of space. But where did the Sun come from? And did it come from the same place as the planets and all the other material in the solar system? To answer these questions, we need to take a much wider view of where the Sun is in space.

ASTEROID Any of the many small objects within the solar system.

COMET A small object, often described as being like a dirty snowball, that appears to be very bright in the night sky and has a long tail when it approaches the Sun.

MASS The amount of matter in an object.

MOON The name generally given to any large natural satellite of a planet.

ORBIT The path followed by one object as it tracks around another.

PLANET Any of the large bodies that orbit the Sun.

SPACE Everything beyond the Earth's atmosphere.

STAR A large ball of gases that radiates light. The star nearest the Earth is the Sun.

To find out about the planets in our solar system see Volume 3: *Earth and Moon*, Volume 4: *Rocky planets*, and Volume 5: *Gas giants*.

▶ An artist's impression of coronal mass ejections leaving the Sun (see page 35). They are the cause of the solar wind (see page 38).

The Milky Way

The UNIVERSE is made of clusters of stars called GALAXIES. The region of space containing the Sun is known as the MILKY WAY Galaxy. The Milky Way itself is a large collection of perhaps 200 billion stars, some of which are far bigger than our Sun.

The Milky Way is about 1,000,000,000,000,000,000 km (about 100,000 LIGHT-YEARS or about 30 KILOPARSECS) across. The space PROBE that has given us the most information about the solar system is called VOYAGER. Voyager travels at 17.3 km/s. It would take Voyager over 1,700,000,000 years to cross the Milky Way Galaxy.

Another way to think about the galaxy's size is to know that it takes about 8 minutes for light from the Sun to reach the Earth. In comparison, the Sun's nearest known stellar neighbor is a DWARF STAR called Proxima Centauri, which is about 4.3 light-years away.

The Milky Way is a SPIRAL GALAXY—it has a number of spiraling arms that lead away from the main mass of the galaxy, which is contained in a central bulge.

A spiral galaxy contains stars at all stages of development. In the center the stars are all of different ages. But on the spiral arms we only find new, or relatively young, stars. The Sun lies about 8 kiloparsecs from the center on what is known as the Sagittarius (spiral) arm of the Milky Way.

DWARF STAR A star that shines with a brightness that is average or below.

GALAXY A system of stars and interstellar matter within the universe.

KILOPARSEC A unit of a thousand parsecs. A parsec is the unit used for measuring the largest distances in the universe.

LIGHT-YEAR The distance traveled by light through space in one Earth year, or 63,240 astronomical units.

LOCAL GROUP The Milky Way, the Magellanic Clouds, the Andromeda Galaxy, and over 20 other relatively near galaxies.

MILKY WAY The spiral galaxy in which our star and solar system are situated.

PROBE An unmanned spacecraft designed to explore our solar system and beyond.

SPIRAL GALAXY A galaxy that has a core of stars at the center of long curved arms made of even more stars arranged in a spiral shape.

UNIVERSE The entirety of everything there is; the cosmos.

VOYAGER A pair of U.S. space probes designed to provide detailed information about the outer regions of the solar system.

For more on Voyager see "Outer worlds" in Volume 6: *Journey into space.*

▼ We cannot see the whole Milky Way because we are inside it. But this shows roughly where the Sun lies within it.

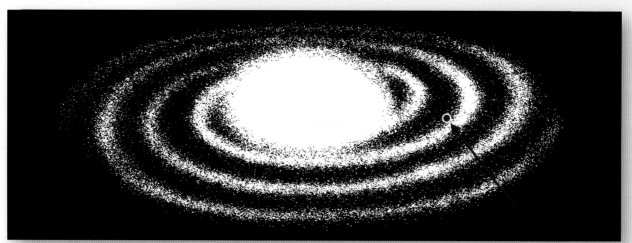

▲ We see our galaxy, the Milky Way, from the side because we are inside it. In this picture the central bulge shows white, and the spiral arms glow less intensely. The white smudges to the lower right are the Magellanic Cloud neighboring galaxies.

For more on galaxies and the Magellanic Clouds see Volume 1: *How the universe works*.

▶ Our nearest neighbors, also known as the **LOCAL GROUP**, account for most of the stars you can see on a clear night with the naked eye. This picture shows a few of them.

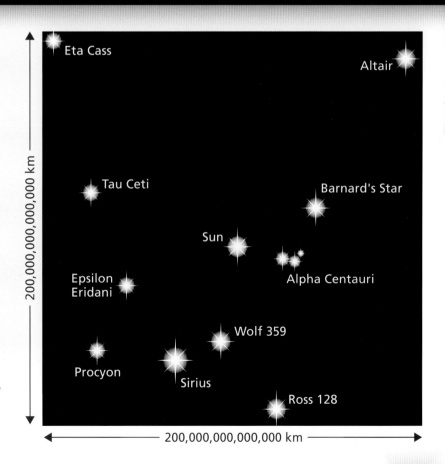

The birth of the Sun

All galaxies contain a huge amount of interstellar ("between star") gas and dust. This material is mainly hydrogen **ATOMS** and hydrogen **MOLECULES**, which are the building blocks of all stars.

Space contains not just the things we can see through powerful optical or **RADIO TELESCOPES**. It also is made up of things we cannot see, such as waves of **RADIATION** (energy).

It is likely that such waves of energy move right through the galaxies. You can think of these waves as being like the ripples created in a pond when someone drops a pebble into the water. As the ripples pass by, the waves do not disturb the main features of the galaxy, such as the stars. They are anchored in place because they are too large to be disturbed by energy waves. But the interstellar cloud is stirred much more easily by **GRAVITY** waves, and its gases and dust can be made to move closer together in some places. When this happens, the gravity of the material starts to pull itself together. This sets in place a train of events that will lead to the formation of a star.

The fuel for a star

Everything about the Sun relies on one important process: the change in energy that occurs as a result of nuclear reactions within it. The main process is nuclear **FUSION**. In it electrons (negatively charged particles) are separated from the **NUCLEUS** of the atom (which is called ionization), and then the central positively charged parts of atoms called protons fuse together. During these reactions the protons in the nuclei of hydrogen atoms fuse to produce protons of helium atoms.

It is the immense gravity inside the Sun that creates the **PRESSURE** that allows fusion reactions to occur in the **CORE**. This intense reaction releases more energy per unit of mass than anything else that happens in the universe.

▲ The Stingray Nebula, the youngest known planetary nebula. A bright central star is in the middle of the green ring of gas. Its companion star is at the top left.

Colors shown are actual colors emitted by nitrogen (red), oxygen (green), and hydrogen (blue).

It is thought that the gas giants (as well as the Sun and even the rocky planets) were formed from such a nebula.

For more on the life cycle of stars see Volume 1: *How the universe works*.

A hydrogen atom weighs 1.0078 **ATOMIC MASS UNITS**, but a helium atom weighs 4.0026. So, as four hydrogen atoms lose their electrons and then fuse into a helium atom, there is some mass left over.

Einstein showed that mass and energy are related by the formula:

$$e = mc^2$$

where **e** = energy, **m** = mass, **c** = the speed of light In the Sun's nuclear reactions about five million tonnes of **MATTER** are converted into energy every second. Put another way, every second about 700,000,000 tonnes of hydrogen are converted to about 695,000,000 tonnes of helium, leaving 5,000,000 tonnes of energy in the form of radiation. The Sun's resulting energy output is 386 billion billion megawatts.

This energy is emitted in various forms of light (**ULTRAVIOLET** light, **X-RAYS**, visible light, **INFRARED** light) and microwaves and **RADIO WAVES**. The Sun also emits energized particles (**NEUTRINOS**, protons) that make up the solar wind (see page 38). These various forms of energy strike Earth, where they warm the planet, drive our weather, and provide energy for life. We are not harmed by most of the radiation or solar wind because the Earth's **ATMOSPHERE** protects us.

The life of a star

A star like the Sun can continue to shine as a result of fusion reactions for as long as there is hydrogen left as a fuel. Gravity keeps pulling the hydrogen together, but the fusion reaction creates searingly hot gas, which tries to expand. The balance of forces keeps the star a stable size with little variation in its brightness for much of its life. During all of this time the star looks similar to the majority of others in a galaxy and is said to belong to the **MAIN SEQUENCE**. If it is of modest size, like the Sun, most of its life is spent this way.

Such stars, including the Sun, have enormously long lives. Much bigger stars are brighter but burn up faster and have shorter lives.

ATMOSPHERE The envelope of gases that surrounds the Earth and other bodies in the universe.

ATOM The smallest particle of an element.

ATOMIC MASS UNIT A measure of the mass of an atom or molecule.

CORE The central region of a body.

FUSION The joining of atomic nuclei to form heavier nuclei.

GRAVITY The force of attraction between bodies.

INFRARED Radiation with a wavelength that is longer than red light.

MAIN SEQUENCE The 90% of stars in the universe that represent the mature phase of stars with small or medium mass.

MATTER Anything that exists in physical form.

MOLECULE A group of two or more atoms held together by chemical bonds.

NEUTRINOS An uncharged fundamental particle that is thought to have no mass.

NUCLEUS (pl. **NUCLEI**) The centermost part of something, the core.

PRESSURE The force per unit area.

RADIATION The transfer of energy in the form of waves (such as light and heat) or particles (such as from radioactive decay of a material).

RADIO TELESCOPE A telescope that is designed to detect radio waves rather than light waves.

RADIO WAVES A form of electromagnetic radiation, like light and heat. Radio waves have a longer wavelength than light waves.

ULTRAVIOLET A form of radiation that is just beyond the violet end of the visible spectrum and so is called "ultra" (more than) violet. At the other end of the visible spectrum is "infra" (less than) red.

X-RAY An invisible form of radiation that has extremely short wavelengths just beyond the ultraviolet.

The life and death of the Sun

The Danish astronomer Ejnar Hertzsprung and the U.S. astronomer Henry Norris Russell both developed charts that can be used to show the life of a star such as the Sun.

The chart on page 11 plots temperature against brightness (luminosity) for the life cycle of the Sun.

Following the diagram around from point A shows the changes that might occur with our Sun.

Nuclear **FUSION** begins at point A. This is the birth of the Sun. The Sun then enters a long period as a yellow main-sequence star, during which time it gets slightly brighter. This stage may last for the best part of 10 billion years, the majority of the life of the star. Since the Sun is 4.5 billion years old, it is currently about halfway between points A and B. The Sun's surface temperature is about 6,000°C.

When the hydrogen in the core of the Sun has been used up, fusion in the shell around the core will begin. The Sun will increase in size to nearly half as big again as it is now. This is point C. The Sun won't have gotten any hotter; but because it is burning hydrogen in its shell and not in its core, it will be about twice as bright as it is now. It will be beginning its **RED GIANT** phase.

Perhaps 1 to 2 billion years after point C has been reached, the Sun will have grown to over three times its current size and will have reached point D. But it will start to get slightly cooler, and its surface temperature will be about 4,300°C. At this point the Sun will be a huge orange-red disk as seen from Earth.

The increased **RADIATION** from the Sun will have increased the temperature of the Earth by 100°C, **EVAPORATING** all of the oceans and destroying all life.

The Sun will then begin to grow quickly, swelling to a size that may reach as far as the Earth. At first it will seem as though the Sun fills half the sky. This huge Sun will melt the surface of the Earth, which will return to being covered in **MOLTEN** rock (as it was when the solar system formed). Then it will fill the entire sky, vaporizing first the planet Mercury, then the planet Venus, and then the Earth. We have reached point E, and the inner rocky planets such as the Earth will be no more.

BLACK DWARF A degenerate star that has cooled so that it is now not visible.

EVAPORATE The change in state from liquid to a gas.

FUSION The joining of atomic nuclei to form heavier nuclei.

MOLTEN Liquid, suggesting that it has changed from a solid.

PLANETARY NEBULA A compact ring or oval nebula that is made of material thrown out of a hot star.

RADIATION The transfer of energy in the form of waves (such as light and heat) or particles (such as from radioactive decay of a material).

RED GIANT A cool, large, bright star at least 25 times the diameter of our Sun.

SOLAR WIND The flow of tiny charged particles (called plasma) outward from the Sun.

WHITE DWARF Any star originally of low mass that has reached the end of its life.

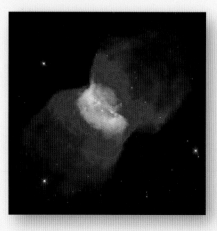

▼ The red giant phase that the Sun might go through (as shown by the Butterfly Nebula).

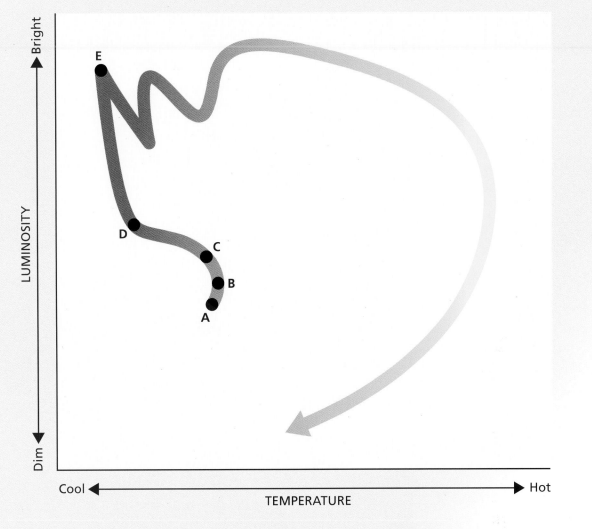

Bright

Dim

LUMINOSITY

E

D

C

B

A

Cool ◄──────────────────────► Hot

TEMPERATURE

▲ The Hertzsprung-Russell diagram for the Sun.

Now the star will explode. The core will get hot enough to fuse the helium into carbon. About a third of the Sun will be thrown out into space. This will create a **PLANETARY NEBULA**, and a giant **SOLAR WIND** will develop around the Sun.

The Sun will get hotter for a while, then collapse down to be a **WHITE DWARF**, getting smaller, dimmer, and cooler. It will only be about half of the mass of the present Sun, but it will be much denser. Cooling and dimming, the Sun will form into a **BLACK DWARF** with no light of its own left. It will be on its own in space, the planets having been destroyed long before.

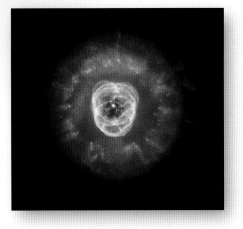

▲ The planetary nebula phase that the Sun might go through (as shown by the Eskimo Nebula).

2: THE SUN

The Sun is called a G2V star. G2 means that it is one of the second hottest stars in the (yellow) G class. V tells us that it is a **MAIN SEQUENCE**, or **DWARF STAR**, which is the most common kind of star. Dwarf, however, does not mean that the Sun is itself a small star. In fact, it is within the top 5% of stars in its neighborhood and in the top 10% of stars by **MASS** in our galaxy. It is simply not one of the **BLUE GIANTS**.

Why the Sun appears so bright

It is difficult to imagine some of the properties of the Sun. For example, it is a mass of gas so hot that it lights up the sky. It contains no liquid or solid at all.

The temperature at the center of the Sun measures about 15,000,000°C, but it is "only" 6,000°C at the "surface." Because we only see the surface, we see the Sun at a color appropriate to 6,000°C—as a yellow-white color.

The surface we see, and which we might take to be some kind of hot solid, is made entirely of gaseous **ATOMS**, mainly hydrogen, which heave around and constantly change shape. Gases also exist in a Sun "atmosphere" beyond the surface.

So, there is nothing special about our Sun. It is a yellow star known as a dwarf star. To us it is immensely bright, but that is simply because we are—at 149,600,000 km—astronomically so close to it.

▲ The constantly changing surface of the Sun.

The Sun gives evidence of rotation

▶ At first glance the solar disk is featureless except for sunspots, visible on these images as dark blemishes.

By tracing the apparent path of sunspots across the solar disk from one day to the next, solar astronomers in the early 17th century could demonstrate that the Sun rotates. They could also estimate the length of the solar day at about 27 Earth days. The largest sunspots or sunspot groups are visible to the naked eye.

The next closest star (Proxima Centauri) is a quarter of a million times farther away. Because brightness decreases with the square of distance from the Earth, this star appears to be 62 billion times less bright than the Sun.

The brightness of the Sun is described by its **MAGNITUDE**. The lower the number, the brighter the star. From the Earth the Sun appears to have a magnitude of –26.8 and so is the brightest thing in the sky. But its absolute magnitude (the star's true brightness if all of the stars were the same distance from Earth) is just 4.8. Thus it is, in reality, not a very bright object. By contrast, a bright star, such as Betelgeuse, has an absolute magnitude of –9 and can be seen clearly even though it is 310 light-years away.

How the Sun moves in space

At 16° latitude the Sun spins on its **AXIS** once every 25.4 days. This is taken as the standard for solar rotation. But, because the Sun is made of fluid gas, and not solid rock like the Earth, not all of it rotates at the same speed. Gas near the poles takes 36 days to rotate.

The Sun's axis is tilted at about 7.25° to the axis of the Earth's **ORBIT**. That is why astronomers can see more of the Sun's northern polar region each September and more of its southern region in March.

ATOM The smallest particle of an element.

AXIS (pl. **AXES**) The line around which a body spins.

BLUE GIANT A young, extremely bright and hot star of very large mass that has used up all its hydrogen and is no longer in the main sequence. When a blue giant ages, it becomes a red giant.

DWARF STAR A star that shines with a brightness that is average or below.

MAGNITUDE A measure of the brightness of a star. The apparent magnitude is the brightness of a celestial object as seen from the Earth. The absolute magnitude is the standardized brightness measured as though all objects were the same distance from the Earth.

MAIN SEQUENCE The 90% of stars in the universe that represent the mature phase of stars with small or medium mass.

MASS The amount of matter in an object.

ORBIT The path followed by one object as it tracks around another.

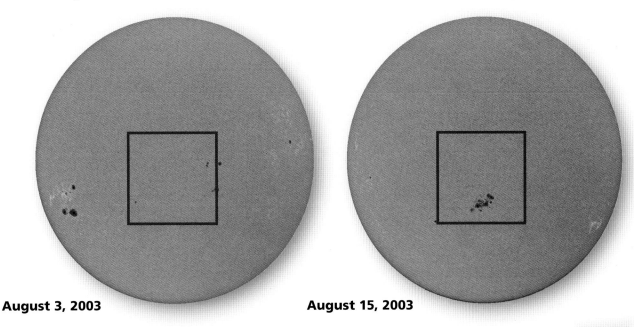

August 3, 2003   **August 15, 2003**

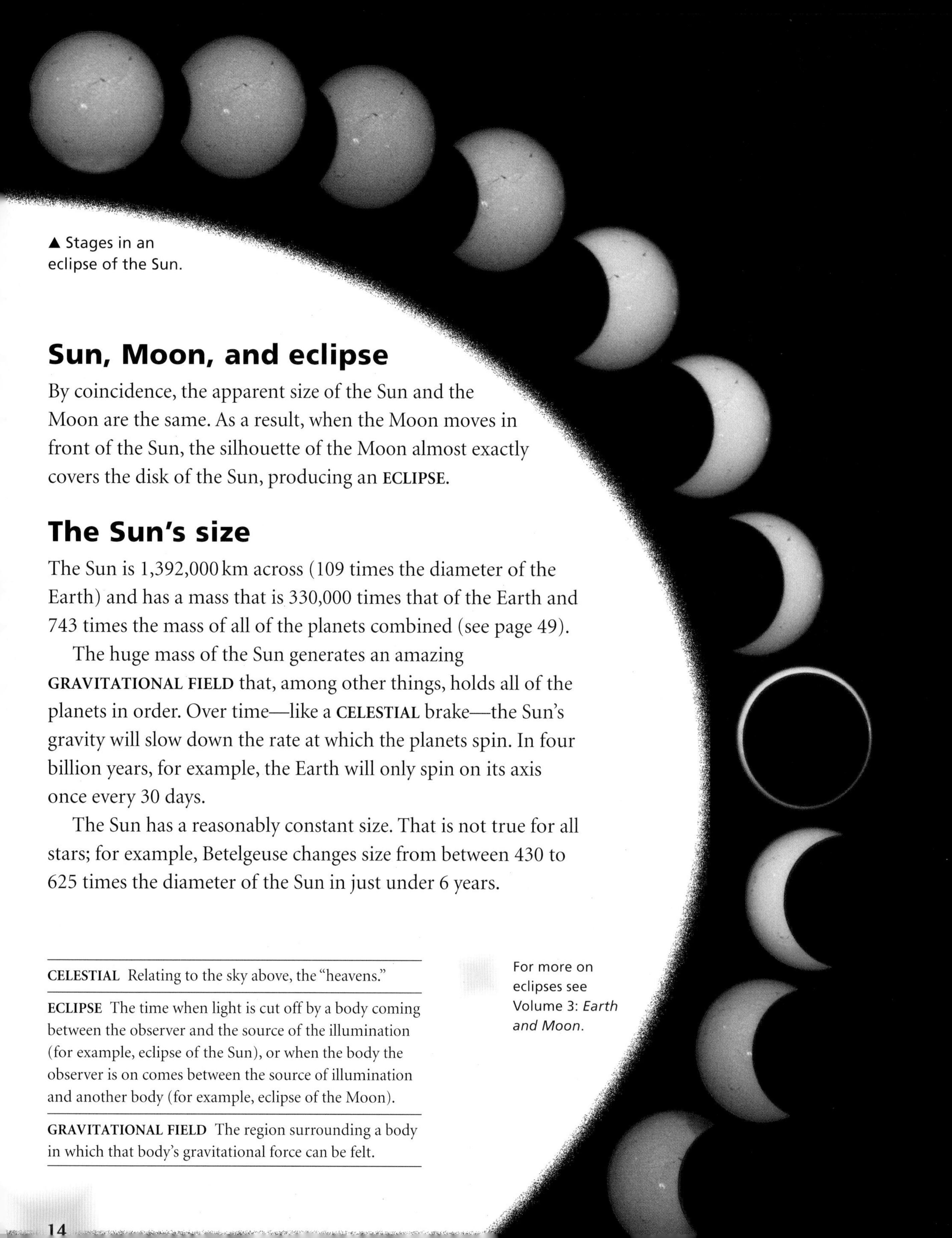

▲ Stages in an
eclipse of the Sun.

Caption below top image:

▲ Stages in an
eclipse of the Sun.

Sun, Moon, and eclipse

By coincidence, the apparent size of the Sun and the
Moon are the same. As a result, when the Moon moves in
front of the Sun, the silhouette of the Moon almost exactly
covers the disk of the Sun, producing an ECLIPSE.

The Sun's size

The Sun is 1,392,000 km across (109 times the diameter of the
Earth) and has a mass that is 330,000 times that of the Earth and
743 times the mass of all of the planets combined (see page 49).

The huge mass of the Sun generates an amazing
GRAVITATIONAL FIELD that, among other things, holds all of the
planets in order. Over time—like a CELESTIAL brake—the Sun's
gravity will slow down the rate at which the planets spin. In four
billion years, for example, the Earth will only spin on its axis
once every 30 days.

The Sun has a reasonably constant size. That is not true for all
stars; for example, Betelgeuse changes size from between 430 to
625 times the diameter of the Sun in just under 6 years.

CELESTIAL Relating to the sky above, the "heavens."

ECLIPSE The time when light is cut off by a body coming
between the observer and the source of the illumination
(for example, eclipse of the Sun), or when the body the
observer is on comes between the source of illumination
and another body (for example, eclipse of the Moon).

GRAVITATIONAL FIELD The region surrounding a body
in which that body's gravitational force can be felt.

For more on
eclipses see
Volume 3: *Earth
and Moon*.

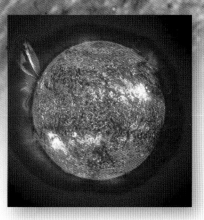

◄▲ Large eruptive prominence
(see pages 33–35), with an image
of the Earth added for size
comparison. This prominence is
particularly large and looping,
extending over 35 Earths out from
the Sun. Erupting prominences
(when directed toward Earth) can
affect communications, navigation
systems, even power grids, while
also producing auroras visible in
the night skies (see page 45).

The Sun's gravity

The Sun's **GRAVITATIONAL FIELD** is so strong that there is a great tendency for the Sun to collapse in on itself. That does not happen because of the huge **PRESSURE** exerted against **GRAVITY** by the burning **ATOMS** in the **CORE**, which always want to expand.

It is believed that the gases at the center of the Sun are squashed to a **DENSITY** six times as great as the atoms in the core of the Earth and exert an outward pressure that is ten thousand times as strong as the atoms in the center of the Earth.

The gases in the core behave as though they were a solid body, although they are still a gas. The core, the inner 25% of the Sun's **RADIUS**, has a pressure of 250 billion Earth **ATMOSPHERES**.

Modeling the Sun

How is it that we know anything at all about the inside of the Sun? In part, this is entirely theory, with scientists making up models in which they assume the Sun has certain properties, and then testing the model on a computer to see if it behaves as the Sun does. If it does not, they tweak the data and try again.

But knowledge of the Sun is also obtained in the same kind of way we find out about the deep regions of the Earth—just by listening to the way the surface vibrates and studying the pattern of vibrations. On Earth the vibrations are either set up by explosions or by **EARTHQUAKES**. In the case of the Sun information has been gathered about the way its surface shakes (see page 32). This study is called **HELIOSEISMOLOGY**.

Scientists can also find out a great deal about the composition of the Sun by looking at the light it gives out. Every **ELEMENT**, such as sodium and calcium, burns with a unique color. You see this, for example, when a piece of calcium is burned in a flame.

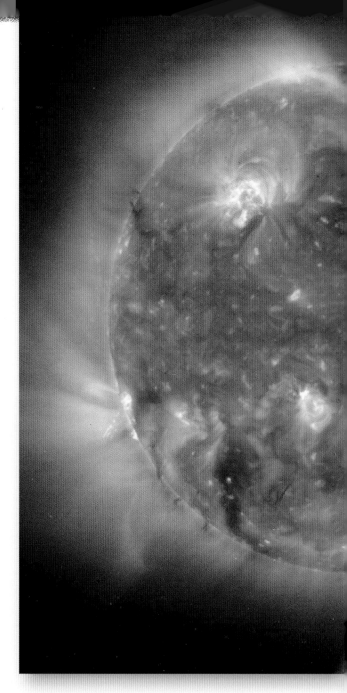

▲ This picture is a combination of images obtained by looking at the **RADIATION** the Sun emits in different wavelengths of **ULTRAVIOLET** light. The result shows features that we could not see in visible light.

Notice the **PLASMA** being released from the surface and following curved lines. These flows are controlled by the **MAGNETISM** of the Sun. Differences in brightness on the surface show where energy is reaching it more effectively in some places than in others.

ATMOSPHERE The envelope of gases that surrounds the Earth and other bodies in the universe.

ATOM The smallest particle of an element.

CORE The central region of a body.

DENSITY A measure of the amount of matter in a space.

EARTHQUAKE The shock waves produced by the sudden movement of two pieces of brittle crust.

ELEMENT A substance that cannot be decomposed into simpler substances by chemical means.

GRAVITATIONAL FIELD The region surrounding a body in which that body's gravitational force can be felt.

GRAVITY The force of attraction between bodies.

HELIOSEISMOLOGY The study of the internal structure of the Sun by modeling the Sun's patterns of internal shock waves.

MAGNETISM An invisible force that has the property of attracting iron and similar metals.

PLASMA A collection of charged particles that behaves something like a gas. It can conduct an electric charge and be affected by magnetic fields.

PRESSURE The force per unit area.

RADIATION The transfer of energy in the form of waves (such as light and heat) or particles (such as from radioactive decay of a material).

RADIUS (pl. **RADII**) The distance from the center to the outside of a circle or sphere.

ULTRAVIOLET A form of radiation that is just beyond the violet end of the visible spectrum and so is called "ultra" (more than) violet. At the other end of the visible spectrum is "infra" (less than) red.

Scientists can analyze the pattern of colors. Each element has a unique "fingerprint" of light. By analyzing the Sun's light and how brightly it shines at certain wavelengths, it was possible in 1925 for Cecilia Payne to discover not only that the Sun consists mainly of hydrogen and helium, but that the proportions are nine to one.

Helium, incidentally, was first discovered in the Sun—at that time it had not been found in nature on Earth. As a result, it was named for the Greek word for the Sun—*helios*.

Later analysis showed that the Sun also contains small amounts of most other elements, especially carbon, nitrogen, oxygen, magnesium, silicon, and iron, just like most parts of the universe.

A slice through the Sun

The Sun is made of three zones where gases are highly concentrated. They are the core, the radiative zone, and the convective zone.

Beyond them the gases are less dense. We call the less dense region the atmosphere of the Sun.

Chromosphere

Umbra of sunspot
(see pages 26–28)

Penumbra of sunspot
(see pages 26–28)

Hottest regions show where photons are reaching the surface most quickly.

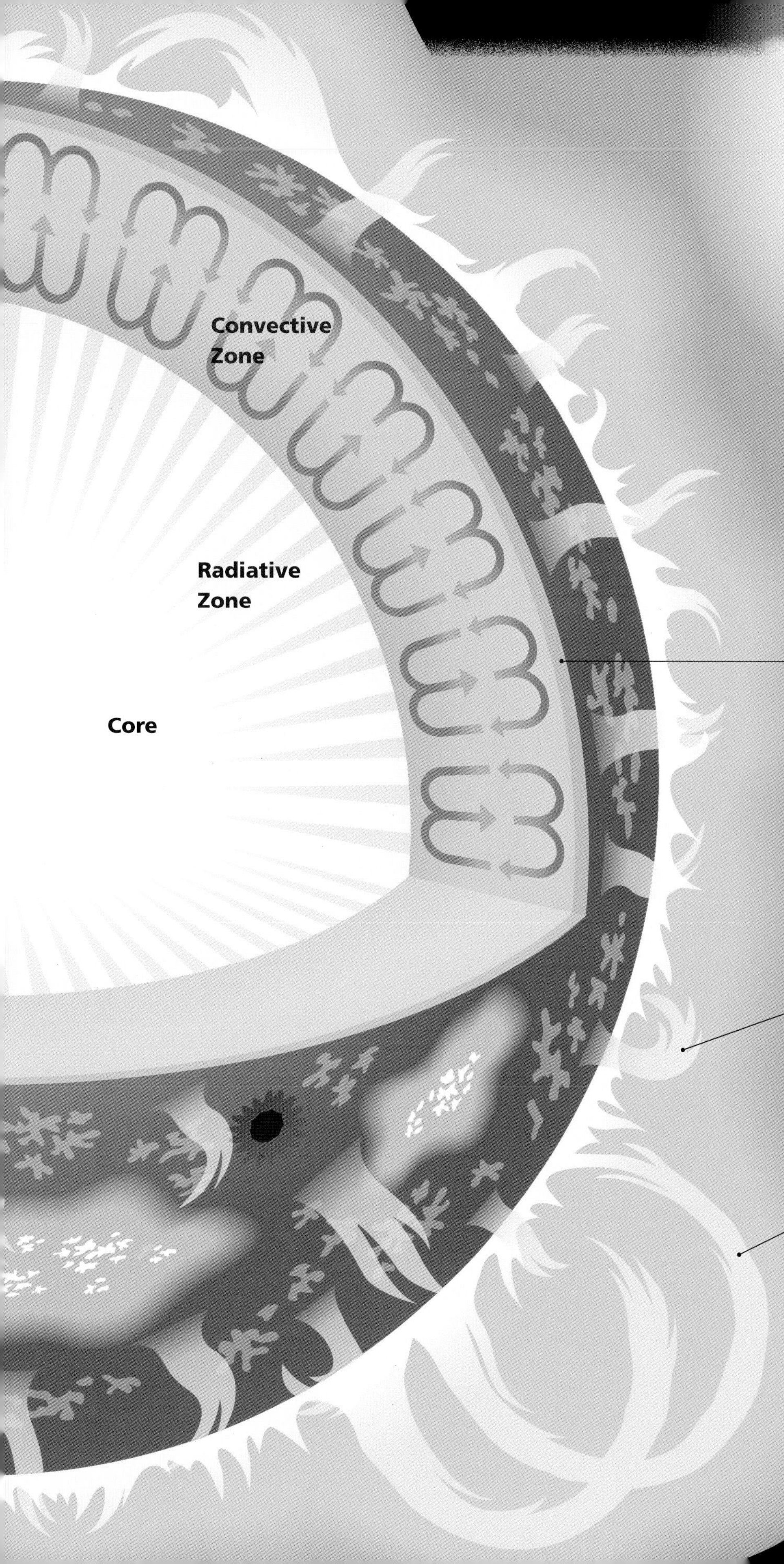

◀ This diagram shows a slice through the Sun. You can see the core (page 21), the radiative zone (page 21), the convective zone (page 22), and the photosphere (pages 23–26) through the chromosphere (page 32) to the corona (pages 35–37).

Convective Zone

Radiative Zone

Core

Corona

Photosphere

Solar flare
(see pages 32–33)

Solar prominence
(see pages 33–34)

The SOHO satellite

Many of the pictures in this book were taken from the SOHO (Solar and Heliospheric Observatory) satellite.

SOHO is designed to study the internal structure of the Sun, its extensive outer atmosphere, and the origin of the solar wind (page 38).

SOHO was launched on December 2, 1995. Large radio dishes around the world, which form the **NASA** deep space network, are used to track the spacecraft.

SOHO is made up of two modules (sections). The service module forms the lower portion of the spacecraft and provides power, thermal control, guidance, and telecommunications for the whole spacecraft as well as support for the **SOLAR PANELS**. The **PAYLOAD** module sits above it and houses all the scientific instruments.

With the solar panels deployed, the satellite is 9.5 m across. SOHO is located 1.5 million kilometers sunward of the Earth.

The core

At the center of the Sun is a region called the core. It is where much of the MATTER of the star is transformed by FUSION from hydrogen to helium, and also where energy is released (see pages 8–9).

The radiative zone

The radiative zone is the region outside the core. It reaches through 55% of the Sun's radius. In this zone the energy from the core is carried outward by particles of energy called PHOTONS.

In the incredibly dense matter within the Sun each photon, once created, moves about 1 MICRON before being absorbed by a gas MOLECULE. The absorption of the photon heats up the gas molecule, and that makes it reemit another photon. The new photon then travels another micron before it, too, is absorbed.

The process of producing photons and absorbing them happens all the way through the radiative zone. By the time a photon has reached the outside of the radiative zone, its predecessors have collided with gas molecules between 10^{19} (ten with 19 zeros after it) and 10^{25} (ten with 25 zeros after it) times.

Even at the speed of light a journey involving 10^{19} collisions can take hundreds of thousands to millions of years. So, the light we see from the Sun, which takes 8 minutes to reach us, may actually have been created in the core of the Sun more than tens of millions of years ago!

Each time a photon is absorbed and a new one released, the photon is absorbed and reemitted at lower and lower temperatures. That alters the wavelength of the energy. The result is that although the energy near the core is mainly gamma ray photons, by the time that energy reaches the surface, it is primarily in wavelengths that produce visible light photons.

FUSION The joining of atomic nuclei to form heavier nuclei.

MATTER Anything that exists in physical form.

MICRON A millionth of a meter.

MOLECULE A group of two or more atoms held together by chemical bonds.

NASA The National Aeronautics and Space Administration.

PAYLOAD The spacecraft that is carried into space by a launcher.

PHOTON A particle (quantum) of electromagnetic radiation.

SOLAR PANELS Large flat surfaces covered with thousands of small photoelectric devices that convert solar radiation into electricity.

The convective zone

In the outermost shell of the Sun the temperature drops below 2,000,000°C, and the PLASMA in the Sun's atmosphere becomes too cool and opaque to allow RADIATION to get through it. So, for the last 20% of the way to the surface the energy is carried more by CONVECTION than by radiation.

The process in this zone can be likened to heating a pot of water on a stove. The water is heated at the bottom; and as it is warmed, it becomes less dense than the water above it. As a result, it rises, while neighboring, cooler, more dense water takes its place. This overturning is called convection, and it happens in just the same way near the surface of the Sun—but with gas at a temperature of thousands of degrees. The CONVECTION CURRENTS carry outward to the surface faster than the radiative transfer that occurs in the core and radiative zone.

Why the Sun burns but does not change

The Sun is, at present, about 75% hydrogen and 25% helium by mass (92.1% hydrogen and 7.8% helium by number of atoms).

Although this represents a huge amount of matter being processed and a vast amount of energy released, it is insignificant compared with the mass of the Sun. At the end of its life the Sun will have turned into energy only a tenth of 1% of the matter it began with—most of it will have been converted into hydrogen. The Sun therefore does not burn up and fade away. Its mass remains almost unchanged. Its density, however, can change dramatically, as we have seen in the Sun's life cycle on pages 10–11.

The solar atmosphere

The Sun's atmosphere is made up of several shells of very thin gases surrounding the star. They are the PHOTOSPHERE, the CHROMOSPHERE, and the CORONA.

The photosphere has properties that mean it is the part of the Sun we see. It can therefore be thought of as the skin of the Sun's main body just as much as the lowest part of its atmosphere. The other two shells of gases are virtually invisible to us.

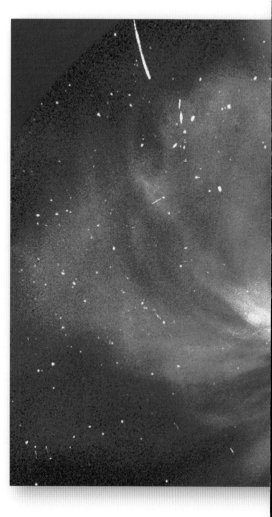

▼ A false-color image of coronal mass ejections of plasma from the Sun into the surrounding corona (see page 35). (False color is used to make the appearance of the ejections more obvious.)

CHROMOSPHERE The shell of gases that makes up part of the atmosphere of a star and lies between the photosphere and the corona.

CONVECTION/CONVECTION CURRENT
The circulating flow in a fluid (liquid or gas) that occurs when it is heated from below.

CORONA (pl. CORONAE) The gases surrounding a star such as the Sun. In the case of the Sun and certain other stars these gases are extremely hot.

PHOTON A particle (quantum) of electromagnetic radiation.

PHOTOSPHERE A shell of the Sun that we regard as its visible surface.

PLASMA A collection of charged particles that behaves something like a gas. It can conduct an electric charge and be affected by magnetic fields.

RADIATION The transfer of energy in the form of waves (such as light and heat) or particles (such as from radioactive decay of a material).

VACUUM A space that is entirely empty.

The photosphere

We see nothing of the inner part of the Sun—what we observe is the slowly spinning lower part of the "atmosphere" called the photosphere.

The photosphere is about 500 km thick, almost like a skin on the surface of the star. Although it is relatively thin, we cannot see through the Sun's photosphere as we can through the Earth's much thicker atmosphere. That is because in the Earth's atmosphere there are few particles to absorb (soak up) light. However, the Sun's photosphere contains particles that absorb all of the light reaching them from the convective zone below, churns them around in their own patterns of convection within itself, and then reemits them. That means we can only see light given out by the outermost layer of particles. Everything below them is obscured. That is why we cannot see through the photosphere. You can get a sense of this if you think about what the Earth looks like in places where cloud cover is high. When such high clouds reflect light, we cannot see through them to the surface.

The photosphere is the place where PHOTONS that began their journey at the core of the Sun eventually escape into space. No longer trapped by the dense gases of the main body of the Sun, they expand; their pressure falls, and so does their temperature. That is why the upper part of the photosphere (what we think of as the "surface" of the Sun) is "only" between 4,000°C and 6,000°C.

Movement in the photosphere

We should think of the photosphere as behaving rather like a liquid. That is despite the fact that the photosphere is actually very "thin," almost a VACUUM, with a density a thousand times less than that of the Earth's atmosphere.

A week in the life of the Sun

▶ To the naked eye the Sun looks like an intensely bright light in the sky. Most of us never imagine that it has a surface full of variation, or that it is constantly changing. In this sequence of pictures of the photosphere—which cover just a week in the life of the Sun—you can see both the variations on the surface and that changes are constantly taking place.

First, notice the surface **GRANULATION** of light and dark blotches (see page 26 for an explanation of this feature). Then, with this background in mind, look to see the way that the bright patches change on this background.

Remember, the Sun spins on its axis once every 25 days (with the rotation from left to right as we see it on these pictures). So, you would expect to see features move across the surface. What you are looking for are changes in the pattern.

Look also at the **SOLAR FLARES** (page 32) that shoot off from the Sun. You can see them where the glow of the Sun meets the blackness of space.

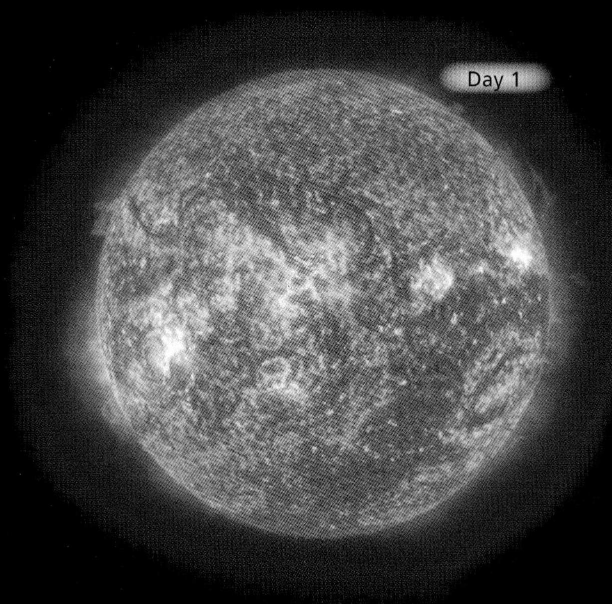

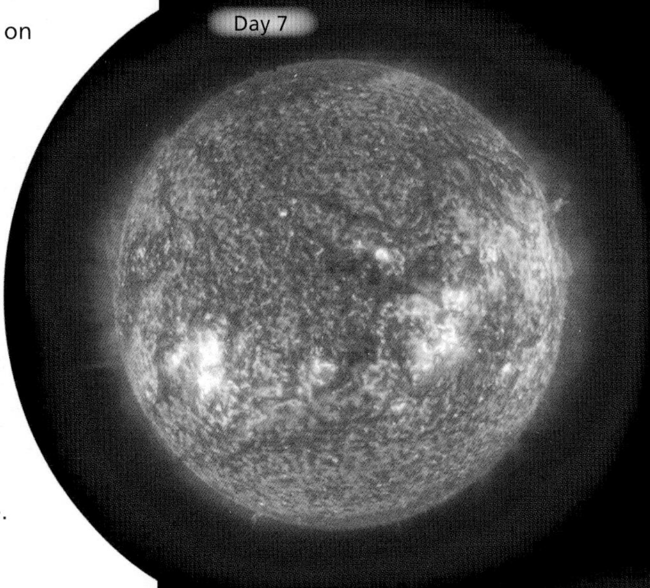

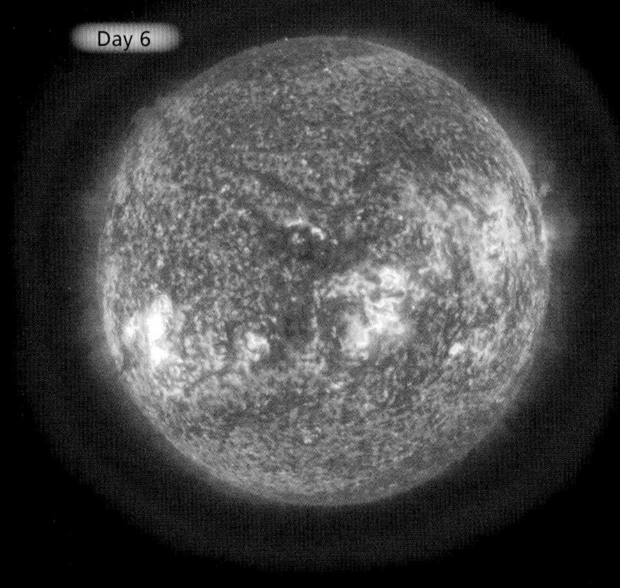

GRANULATION The speckled pattern we see in the Sun's photosphere as a result of convectional overturning of gases.

SOLAR FLARE Any sudden explosion from the surface of the Sun that sends ultraviolet radiation into the chromosphere. It also sends out some particles that reach Earth and disrupt radio communications.

Day 1

Day 7

Day 6

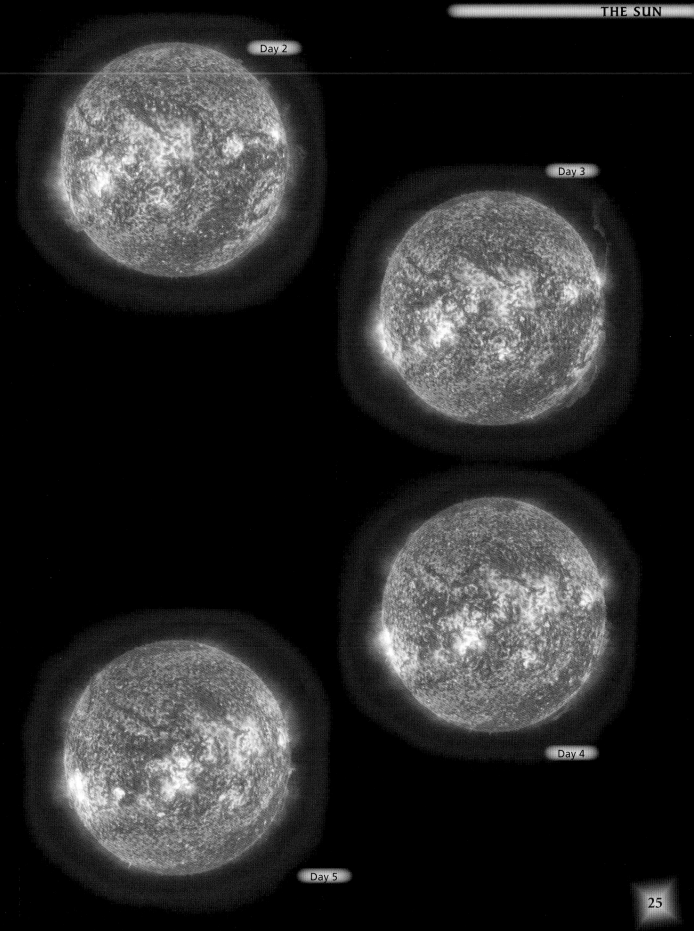

Day 2

Day 3

Day 4

Day 5

Because the photosphere is made of gas, it does not all spin at the same rate, just as our atmosphere does not spin at the same rate as the Earth. However, in the case of the Sun, where the temperature all over the surface is about the same, gases do not move between the **EQUATOR** and the **POLES** as they do on Earth. Instead, bands of gas spin at differing rates depending on their **LATITUDE**. Something similar also happens as thick layers of gases move on the gas giant planets such as Jupiter.

Gases spin fastest at the Sun's equator, making a complete rotation every 25 days. At the poles gases spin more slowly, rotating every 36 days.

Superimposed on this latitudinal spinning are vertical movements in and out of the photosphere. They are **CONVECTION CURRENTS**, and they bring up hotter **IONIZED** gas, or **PLASMA**, from the lower regions of the photosphere and return cooler surface plasma (see page 22). This produces cells about a thousand kilometers across whose speckled surface effect is called **GRANULATION**. Light areas are upwelling currents; dark granules are cooler, downward moving currents.

These cells form and re-form amazingly quickly. A cell might have a life of less than half an hour, and during this time gases move within the cell at up to 300 kilometers each second.

Sunspots

Although we see granulation all over the surface, what catches our attention when we see the Sun at lower magnification are larger features called **SUNSPOTS**. Sunspots were first seen in about A.D 1600.

CONVECTION CURRENTS The circulating flow in a fluid (liquid or gas) that occurs when it is heated from below.

EQUATOR The ring drawn around a body midway between the poles.

GRANULATION The speckled pattern we see in the Sun's photosphere as a result of convectional overturning of gases.

IONIZED Matter that has been converted into small charged particles called ions.

LATITUDE Angular distance north or south of the equator, measured through 90°.

PENUMBRA The part of a sunspot surrounding the umbra.

PLASMA A collection of charged particles that behaves something like a gas. It can conduct an electric charge and be affected by magnetic fields.

POLE The geographic pole is the place where a line drawn along the axis of rotation exits from a body's surface.

SUNSPOT A spiral of gas found on the Sun that is moving slowly upward, and that is cooler than the surrounding gas and so looks darker.

UMBRA The darkest region in the center of a sunspot.

▶ A closeup view of sunspots showing the **UMBRA** (very dark) and **PENUMBRA** (dark) among the granulations of the photosphere.

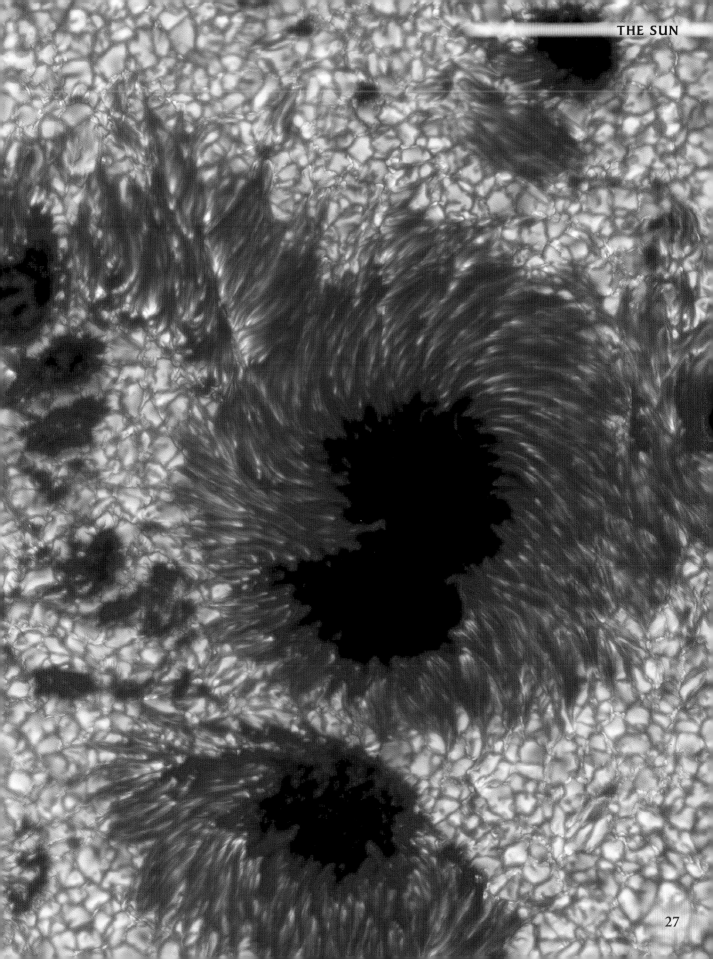

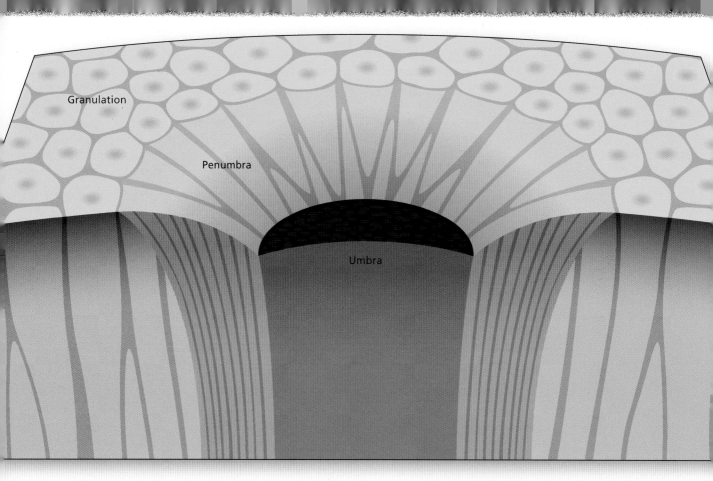

Granulation

Penumbra

Umbra

Sunspots are dark features in the upper photosphere. Because dark indicates cool, sunspots are places where the full upward-flowing energy of the Sun is blocked.

Sunspots are formed by convection currents but on a different scale than granulation. They are often thousands of kilometers across and are also closely connected with the Sun's **MAGNETIC FIELD.** Wherever a sunspot occurs, the magnetic field is preventing the normal amount of convection. As a result, hot materials do not reach the surface as quickly, and so the surface is cooler by about 1,500°C, and therefore darker, than the surroundings.

From this core the magnetic field then spreads out across the spot. The shape of a sunspot is often like an open flower, with a dark central region (called the **UMBRA**) surrounded by a ring of dark "petals" called the **PENUMBRA.**

▲▼ This diagram is a closeup view of a moderately large sunspot. The field of view covers about 60,000 km horizontally and 38,000 km vertically. The diameter of this sunspot is about 16,500 km; the Earth, with an equatorial radius of 6,378 km, would cover up the very dark region (called the umbra) but not the medium-dark region (the penumbra). Sunspots can be quite small (1,500 km diameter) or reach sizes up to 50,000 km.

Sunspots last for weeks and months, then break up into smaller and smaller sunspots.

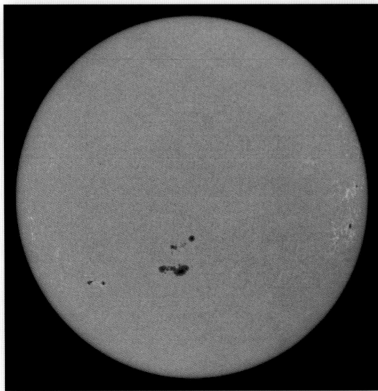

◄▲ Pictures of sunspots. They are constantly changing, so that no two pictures of the Sun are ever the same.

MAGNETIC FIELD The region of influence of a magnetic body.

PENUMBRA The part of a sunspot surrounding the umbra.

UMBRA The darkest region in the center of a sunspot.

Sunspot cycles

Sunspot activity increases and decreases over time all across the Sun, making up an 11-year cycle. At the start of a cycle the number of spots increases, and all spots get bigger, beginning first near the poles, then spreading to the equator to make a pattern that resembles a butterfly.

After about 3 years into the cycle it reaches a stage called the sunspot maximum. Spots do not last through the whole cycle but have a lifetime about the same as the time it takes for the gases at any latitude to go once around the Sun.

At the sunspot maximum there can be 300 spots clustered into about ten groups, although a few groups will contain most of the spots. After this stage the number of sunspots gradually decreases to end the cycle. At the end of the cycle there may be just a few spots left.

▼ Changes in sunspot numbers over the past four centuries. The time of the Little Ice Age corresponded with very low sunspot numbers. No one is yet sure whether this is a coincidence, or if the two features are related.

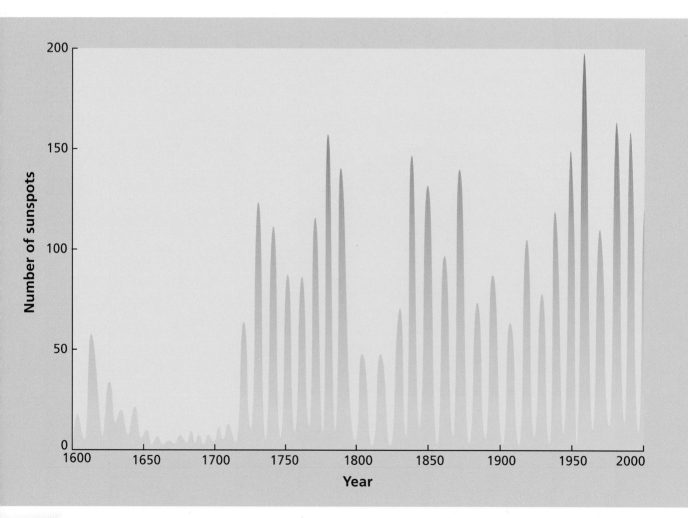

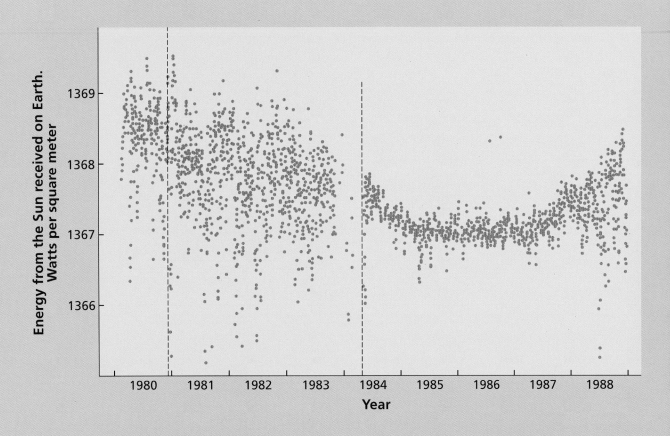

▲ During the Skylab space station missions the variations in energy received on Earth from the Sun were recorded. They showed a cyclic pattern.

For more on Skylab see Volume 7: *Shuttle to Space Station*.

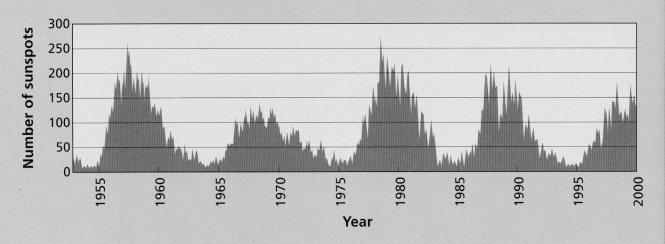

▲ This is how the number of sunspots has changed in recent years. The peaks and troughs show an approximately 11-year cycle. The next minimum will be about 2006.

Sunspot activity has a considerable effect on the Earth. For example, a period of extremely low sunspot activity occurred at the same time as the Little Ice Age (around the 17th century), when glaciers spread out to cover parts of the northern continents. The last sunspot maximum was in 2002.

The chromosphere

Beyond the photosphere (the part of the "atmosphere" of the Sun that we see as a bright yellow disk) lies a small, even thinner part of the atmosphere that shines less brightly. The Sun's atmosphere is faint in visible light but glows brightly in **ULTRAVIOLET** light and in **X-RAYS**. It is pink in color (hence its name **CHROMOSPHERE**); and because it is pale, it can only be seen during an **ECLIPSE**.

The chromosphere is both very thin and very hot, the individual particles reaching temperatures up to 1,000,000°C.

Flares

A sudden release of magnetic energy at speeds of up to 1,500 kilometers per second can sometimes come from a sunspot to produce the most violent event on the Sun's surface—a **SOLAR FLARE**. Flares are closely connected to places where groups of very active sunspots occur.

Flares are invisible in ordinary light and can only be seen with strong colored filters.

Flares occur where tangled **MAGNETIC FIELD** lines meet in the Sun's atmosphere. If magnetic field lines meet going in opposite directions, they produce a magnetic short circuit, called a recombination.

A large flare can release as much energy as the entire Sun normally does. Most of this energy is in the form of **ELECTRONS** and **PROTONS**, and the light emitted is only a secondary effect. The electrons heat up the surface and produce an immensely hot **PLASMA**, which moves out into the outermost atmosphere (the corona, see pages 35–37). That in turn produces X-rays and **RADIO WAVES**.

▲ This is an image taken from a film showing a solar quake. The white, feathery object in the center is the solar flare that caused the quake.

A solar flare is an explosion in the atmosphere of the Sun caused by the tearing and reconnecting of strong magnetic fields. Although moderate in size, this flare released an enormous amount of energy. It produced the shock waves of the solar quake, which can be seen as concentric rings spreading outward from beneath the flare, much like ripples spreading from a rock dropped into a pool of water.

The flare-generated solar quake contained about 40,000 times the energy released in the great earthquake that devastated San Francisco in 1906.

The study of solar quakes is called helioseismology (see page 16).

As the flares run out of energy and cool down, they produce loop **PROMINENCES** as described below.

Flares add considerably to the amount of material being ejected into the corona, produce much of the material flowing outward as the **SOLAR WIND**, and can cause great magnetic shock waves through the solar system. Particle storms produced by flares bathe the Earth in protons.

Prominences

Largely horizontal arcs of **IONIZED** gas are called prominences. Both prominences and the chromosphere are transparent in white light and, except during **TOTAL ECLIPSES**, can only be seen using telescopes with colored filters.

Some prominences only last a short time; others are much longer lasting and are connected to large-scale patterns of **MAGNETISM** within the Sun.

The long-lived prominences are sheetlike in form—the equivalent of solar clouds in the solar atmosphere.

Much more spectacular are prominences produced by solar flares, short-term upward jets of plasma that are extremely violent eruptions of matter from the photosphere. Toward the end of their "lives" they form loop prominences.

Prominences also emit large amounts of ultraviolet rays, gamma rays, and X-rays.

Prominences and spicules (see page 35) are mutually exclusive. Parts of the chromosphere have prominences and no spicules; others have spicules and no prominences.

CHROMOSPHERE The shell of gases that makes up part of the atmosphere of a star and lies between the photosphere and the corona.

ECLIPSE The time when light is cut off by a body coming between the observer and the source of the illumination (for example, eclipse of the Sun), or when the body the observer is on comes between the source of illumination and another body (for example, eclipse of the Moon).

ELECTRONS Negatively charged particles that are parts of atoms.

IONIZED Matter that has been converted into small charged particles called ions.

MAGNETIC FIELD The region of influence of a magnetic body.

MAGNETISM An invisible force that has the property of attracting iron and similar metals.

PLASMA A collection of charged particles that behaves something like a gas. It can conduct an electric charge and be affected by magnetic fields.

PROMINENCE A cloud of burning ionized gas that rises through the Sun's chromosphere into the corona. It can take the form of a sheet or a loop.

PROTONS Positively charged particles from the core of an atom.

RADIO WAVES A form of electromagnetic radiation, like light and heat. Radio waves have a longer wavelength than light waves.

SOLAR FLARE Any sudden explosion from the surface of the Sun that sends ultraviolet radiation into the chromosphere. It also sends out some particles that reach Earth and disrupt radio communications.

SOLAR WIND The flow of tiny charged particles (called plasma) outward from the Sun.

TOTAL ECLIPSE When one body (such as the Moon or Earth) completely obscures the light source from another body (such as the Earth or Moon).

ULTRAVIOLET A form of radiation that is just beyond the violet end of the visible spectrum and so is called "ultra" (more than) violet. At the other end of the visible spectrum is "infra" (less than) red.

X-RAY An invisible form of radiation that has extremely short wavelengths just beyond the ultraviolet.

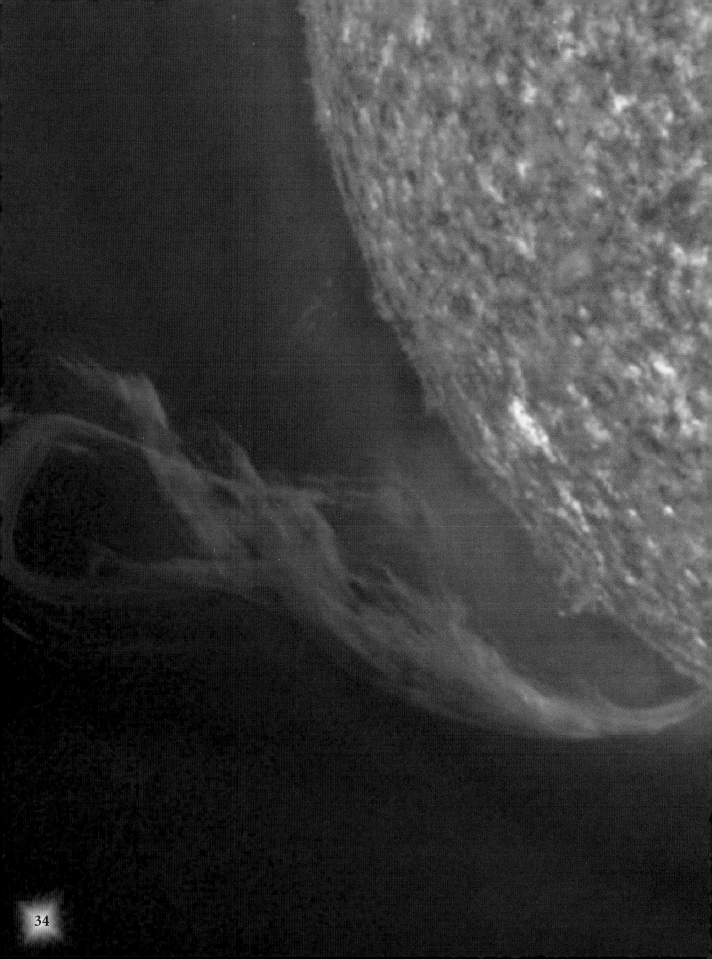

There is a cyclic pattern in the activity of solar prominences, just as there is for sunspots and flares. They rise to a maximum and then subside again over an 11-year cycle.

Spicules

MAGNETISM is responsible for most phenomena in the chromosphere. MAGNETIC FIELDS influence the direction of upward-moving jets of gas that reach up from the photosphere and into the chromosphere. These jets of IONIZED gas are called SPICULES, and they rise about 7,000 km from the photosphere. They are the main sources of the ionized gas that makes up the CORONA (see below).

About 100,000 spicules are sending up material at 20 km a second at any given moment. Any individual spicule has a life of just a few minutes. It then dies and is replaced by another one that leaves the surface at a slightly different position.

The corona

Beyond the chromosphere lies the very, very thin atmosphere called the corona. The dim halo of the corona reaches beyond the planets and eventually extends to the edges of the solar system. We are within the Sun's corona.

The individual particles in the corona are extremely hot, mostly at a million degrees near the Sun and still 200,000°C when they spread out into the region of space around the Earth. However, they also are very scarce, for the corona is the region that we know as space, and space has virtually nothing in it. As a result, to a person in space the corona feels very cold.

CORONAL MASS EJECTIONS are huge magnetic bubbles of PLASMA that erupt from the Sun's corona and travel through space at high speed (for pictures see pages 4, 22–23, and 44). Coronal loops are also found arcing far into the corona (see pages 36–37).

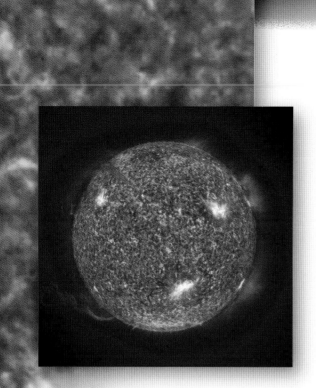

◀▲ A large prominence shooting out near the lower left of the Sun.

CORONA (pl. CORONAE) The gases surrounding a star such as the Sun. In the case of the Sun and certain other stars these gases are extremely hot.

CORONAL MASS EJECTIONS Very large bubbles of plasma escaping into the corona.

IONIZED Matter that has been converted into small charged particles called ions.

MAGNETIC FIELD The region of influence of a magnetic body.

MAGNETISM An invisible force that has the property of attracting iron and similar metals.

PLASMA A collection of charged particles that behaves something like a gas. It can conduct an electric charge and be affected by magnetic fields.

SPICULES Jets of relatively cool gas that move upward through the chromosphere into the corona.

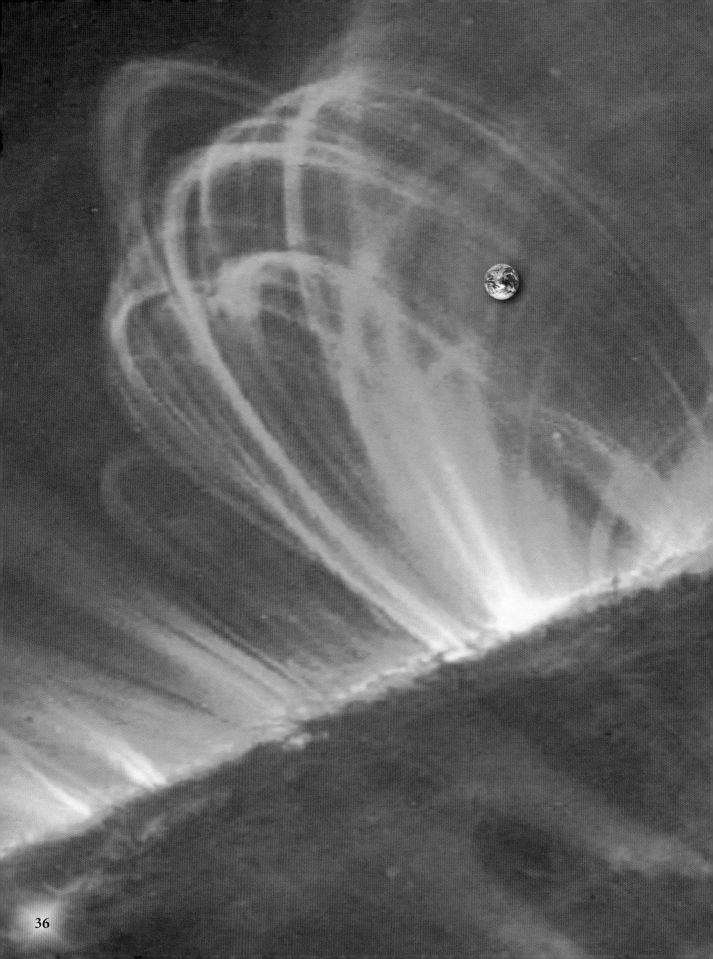

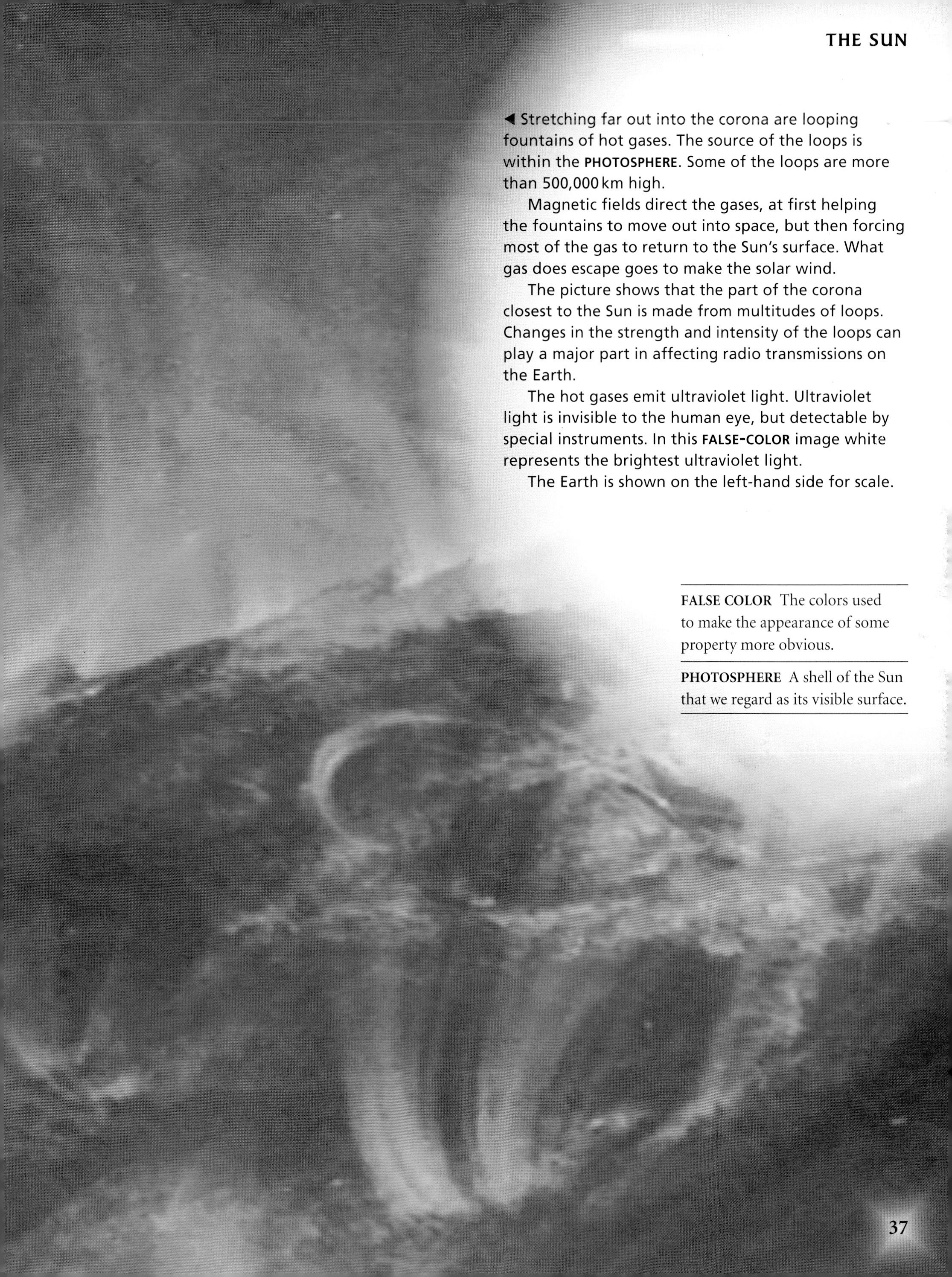

◀ Stretching far out into the corona are looping fountains of hot gases. The source of the loops is within the PHOTOSPHERE. Some of the loops are more than 500,000 km high.

Magnetic fields direct the gases, at first helping the fountains to move out into space, but then forcing most of the gas to return to the Sun's surface. What gas does escape goes to make the solar wind.

The picture shows that the part of the corona closest to the Sun is made from multitudes of loops. Changes in the strength and intensity of the loops can play a major part in affecting radio transmissions on the Earth.

The hot gases emit ultraviolet light. Ultraviolet light is invisible to the human eye, but detectable by special instruments. In this FALSE-COLOR image white represents the brightest ultraviolet light.

The Earth is shown on the left-hand side for scale.

FALSE COLOR The colors used to make the appearance of some property more obvious.

PHOTOSPHERE A shell of the Sun that we regard as its visible surface.

Solar wind

The flow of charged particles (which together are described as **PLASMA**) occurs outward in all directions from the Sun, and it creates the **SOLAR WIND**. The solar wind reaches to the outer regions of the solar system, perhaps traveling beyond **NEPTUNE**.

Particles move outward very quickly within the corona. They start at a speed of up to 700 km per second, then slow down gradually toward the outer edge of the solar system. In the region of the Earth their speed is about 400 km per second—about the distance from New York to Washington, D.C.

The particles in the solar wind have a considerable effect on the Earth because they interact with the Earth's **MAGNETOSPHERE**. They cause a wide range of phenomena, including **RADIO INTERFERENCE** and the auroras (see page 45).

The solar wind also blows the tails of **COMETS** away from the Sun and even has measurable effects on the path of spacecraft. As a result, it has been suggested that by building a sufficiently large solar sail, it would be possible to be carried through the solar system on the solar wind.

COMET A small object, often described as being like a dirty snowball, that appears to be very bright in the night sky and has a long tail when it approaches the Sun.

MAGNETOSPHERE A region in the upper atmosphere, or around a planet, where magnetic phenomena such as auroras are found.

NEPTUNE The eighth planet from the Sun in our solar system and five planets farther away from the Sun than the Earth.

PLASMA A collection of charged particles that behaves something like a gas. It can conduct an electric charge and be affected by magnetic fields.

RADIO INTERFERENCE Reduction in the radio communication effectiveness of the ionosphere caused by sunspots and other increases in the solar wind.

SOLAR WIND The flow of tiny charged particles (called plasma) outward from the Sun.

Solar sail

If you have ever watched a radiometer (a glass bulb with little black and silver panels inside that spin when the Sun shines), you will already be familiar with the idea that the Sun can, in one way or another, send energy across space.

A solar sail works because the Sun sends out particles that form the solar wind. A solar sail catches sunlight. As Newton's **LAWS OF MOTION** tell us: For every action there is an equal and opposite **REACTION**. When **PHOTONS** in the solar wind hit a solar sail, they apply a force to it. The sail applies an equal and opposite force that moves it away from the Sun.

There is no end to the solar wind, and so there is a slight but constant force applied to the sail. The result is that it is constantly **ACCELERATING**. In time sunlight could move a sail faster than any rocket could power a spacecraft.

Such a solar sail would have to have a large area and be made of the lightest material. The low **MASS** is important because acceleration is force divided by mass. The bigger the mass, the smaller the acceleration.

Suitable solar sail material would be metal-coated plastic. Sails could be large disks, or they could have large blades.

ACCELERATE To gain speed.

LAWS OF MOTION Formulated by Sir Isaac Newton, they describe the forces that act on a moving object.

MASS The amount of matter in an object.

PROTONS Positively charged particles from the core of an atom.

REACTION An opposition to a force.

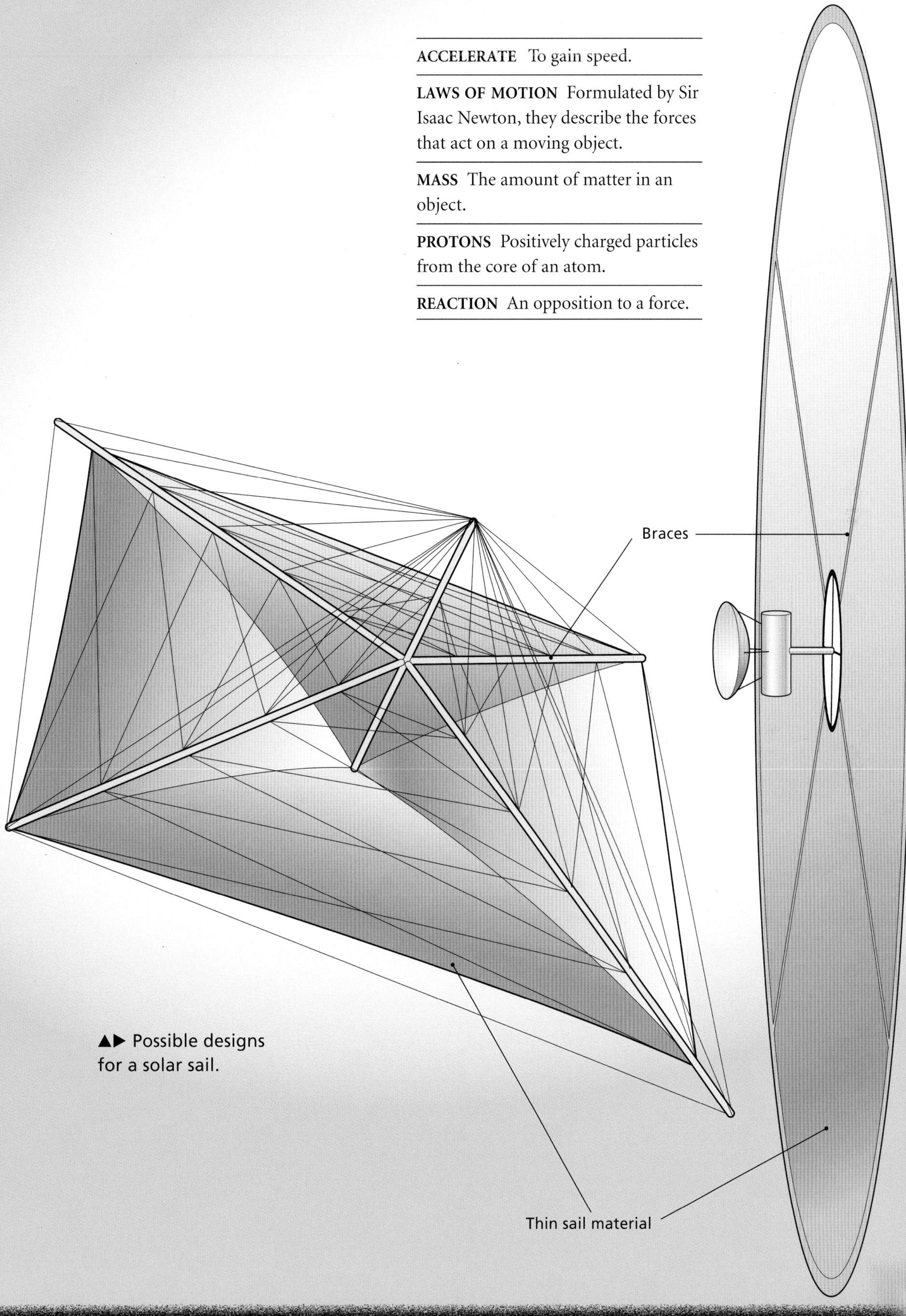

Braces

▲▶ Possible designs for a solar sail.

Thin sail material

▼ In this diagram of the heliosphere the white lines represent the flow of particles, mostly hydrogen ions, in the interstellar wind. They are deflected around the edge of the heliosphere to make the heliopause. The red arrow shows how neutral particles penetrate the heliopause. They are primarily hydrogen and helium atoms, which mostly are not affected by magnetic fields. There are also heavier dust grains. These interstellar neutral particles make up a substantial part of the material found within the heliosphere.

   The edge of the green area shows where the solar wind slows down to less than the speed of sound.

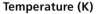

Temperature (K)

1.9x10⁶
6.4x10⁵
2.1x10⁵
7.2x10⁴
2.4x10⁴
8.0x10³

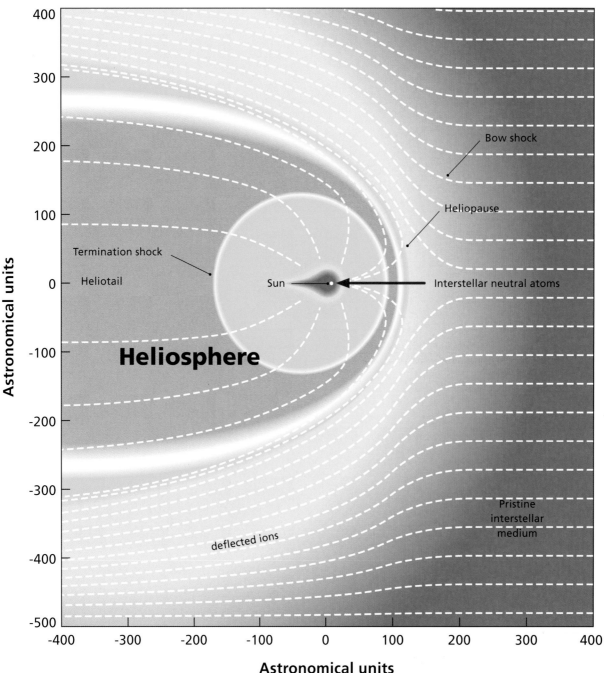

Heliosphere

The **HELIOSPHERE**, also called the magnetosphere, is the region over which the Sun's magnetic influence and **SOLAR WIND** spreads. It is immense and reaches out beyond **PLUTO**. It is like a giant, invisible teardrop-shaped bubble in space.

Because the Sun is continually moving through space, the heliosphere interacts with the surrounding **INTERSTELLAR** medium.

The edge of the heliosphere is called the **HELIOPAUSE**. It is a teardrop-shaped boundary around the Sun that is filled with both a solar magnetic field and the solar wind, which is made of protons and electrons. Ahead of the heliopause there may be bow shock waves similar in pattern to those that form in front of a fast-moving boat or airplane. The long tail of the heliopause may reach 100 **ASTRONOMICAL UNITS** from the Sun.

How the Sun affects the Earth

When we look at the Sun, we might imagine that its main effect is to provide light and heat. However, the Sun sends out **RADIATION** over a much greater range. It also sends out charged particles that form the solar wind.

UV and X-rays

The main forms of radiation in addition to light and heat are **ULTRAVIOLET** (UV) rays and **X-RAYS**. Ultraviolet rays react with oxygen in the air to produce **OZONE**. Ozone absorbs ultraviolet radiation, acting as a natural shield against these rays, which are harmful to living things exposed to them for a long time.

X-rays from the Sun's corona interact with the Earth's upper atmosphere to produce the layer we call the **IONOSPHERE**. The ionosphere helps bounce **RADIO WAVES** and so makes possible long-distance radio.

ASTRONOMICAL UNIT (**AU**) The average distance from the Earth to the Sun (149,597,870 km).

HELIOPAUSE The edge of the heliosphere.

HELIOSPHERE The entire range of influence of the Sun. It extends to the edge of the solar system.

INTERSTELLAR Between the stars.

IONOSPHERE A part of the Earth's atmosphere in which the number of ions (electrically charged particles) is enough to affect how radio waves move.

OZONE A form of oxygen (O_3) with three atoms in each molecule instead of the more usual two (O_2).

PLUTO The ninth planet from the Sun and six planets farther from the Sun than the Earth.

RADIATION The transfer of energy in the form of waves (such as light and heat) or particles (such as from radioactive decay of a material).

RADIO WAVES A form of electromagnetic radiation, like light and heat. Radio waves have a longer wavelength than light waves.

SOLAR WIND The flow of tiny charged particles (called plasma) outward from the Sun.

ULTRAVIOLET A form of radiation that is just beyond the violet end of the visible spectrum and so is called "ultra" (more than) violet. At the other end of the visible spectrum is "infra" (less than) red.

X-RAY An invisible form of radiation that has extremely short wavelengths just beyond the ultraviolet.

Magnetism

The **SOLAR WIND** is made of charged particles, mostly **PROTONS** and **ELECTRONS**.

In the case of planets like **VENUS** and **MARS**, which have no **MAGNETIC FIELD**, the solar wind washes right over them. However, the Earth has a large magnetic field. It spreads out from the Earth in every direction. At a distance of about 10 Earth radii (65,000 km) in the direction of the Sun the **PRESSURE** effect of the magnetic field of the Earth is balanced by the pressure of particles in the solar wind.

Between this point, called the **MAGNETOPAUSE**, and the Earth's surface the Earth's **MAGNETISM** is strong enough to repel most of the solar wind.

ELECTRONS Negatively charged particles that are parts of atoms.

MAGNETIC FIELD The region of influence of a magnetic body.

MAGNETISM An invisible force that has the property of attracting iron and similar metals.

MAGNETOPAUSE The outer edge of the magnetosphere.

MAGNETOSPHERE A region in the upper atmosphere, or around a planet, where magnetic phenomena such as auroras are found.

MARS The fourth planet from the Sun in our solar system and one planet farther away from the Sun than the Earth.

PLASMA A collection of charged particles that behaves something like a gas. It can conduct an electric charge and be affected by magnetic fields.

PRESSURE The force per unit area.

PROTONS Positively charged particles from the core of an atom.

SOLAR WIND The flow of tiny charged particles (called plasma) outward from the Sun.

VENUS The second planet from the Sun and our closest neighbor.

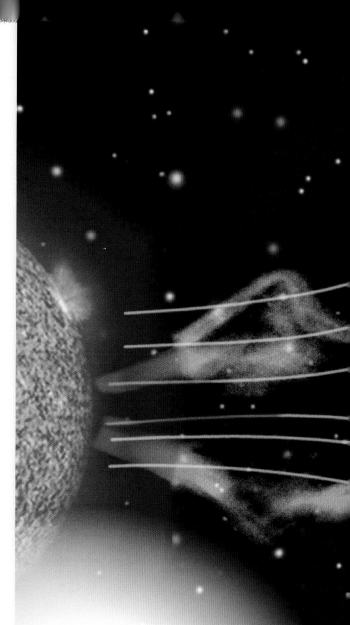

▶ The Sun's magnetic field and its releases of **PLASMA** directly affect Earth and the rest of the solar system. Solar wind shapes the Earth's **MAGNETOSPHERE**. Magnetic storms are illustrated here as they approach Earth. These storms, which occur frequently, can disrupt communications and navigational equipment, damage satellites, and even cause blackouts. The white lines represent the solar wind; the purple line is the bow shock line; and the green lines surrounding the Earth represent its protective magnetosphere. The magnetic cloud of plasma can extend to 48 million kilometers in width by the time it reaches the Earth.

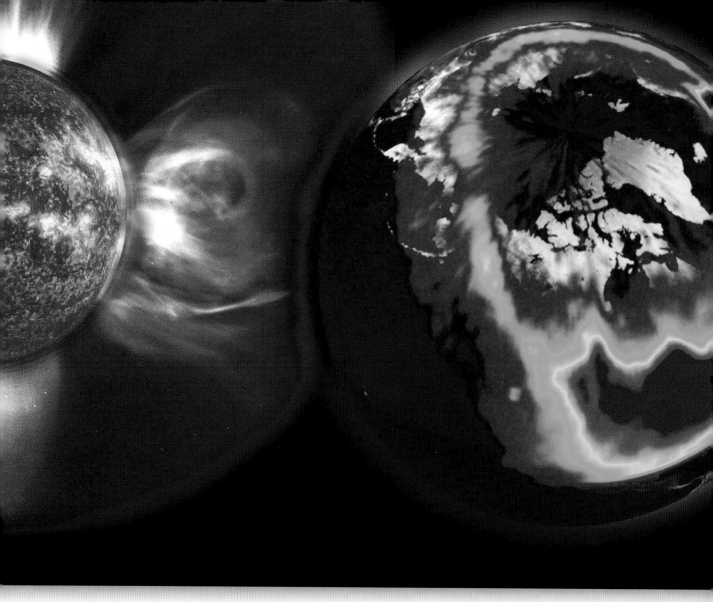

▲ This picture shows how a storm from the Sun (a coronal mass ejection—see page 35) on the left causes charged particles to spread over the Earth (center) and thus produce an aurora (right).

The region where the solar wind is repulsed is called the Earth's **MAGNETOSPHERE**. Like the Sun's heliosphere, it is teardrop shaped.

The solar wind is deflected around the Earth, slightly squashing the Earth's magnetosphere perpendicular to the solar wind. Behind the Earth the Earth's magnetosphere and the solar wind reinforce each other. As a result, the magnetosphere is blunted toward the Sun and has an elongated tail away from the Sun that is more than 1 **ASTRONOMICAL UNIT** in length.

ASTRONOMICAL UNIT (AU) The average distance from the Earth to the Sun (149,597,870 km).

AURORA A region of illumination, often in the form of a wavy curtain, high in the atmosphere of a planet.

ELECTRONS Negatively charged particles that are parts of atoms.

FLUORESCENT Emitting the visible light produced by a substance when it is struck by invisible waves, such as ultraviolet waves.

Auroras

The plasma in the Sun's heliosphere (the solar wind) can leak into the magnetosphere of the Earth. Charged particles thus come down toward the Earth. This causes great turbulence in the magnetosphere, dumping charged particles into the **IONOSPHERE** below it.

The charged particles from the solar wind are carried downward toward the magnetic poles. As they move through the upper atmosphere, they collide with oxygen and nitrogen atoms. The collisions knock electrons away from the atoms. That changes them into charged ions, which then radiate red or greenish-blue light.

When that happens, beautiful displays of charged particles—like natural **FLUORESCENT**-colored drapes—can be seen. They are called **AURORAS**. They are most commonly seen in northern locations such as Anchorage, Alaska, and Iqaluit, Nunavut, Canada. However, during periods of intense solar activity auroras can reach down from the poles to the midlatitudes and have occasionally been seen as far south as 40°N.

When a major **SOLAR FLARE** produces bursts of **PROTON** and **ELECTRON** particles, they can also change the Earth's magnetic field, disrupting radio communications and even affecting the long-distance transmission of high-voltage electricity.

IONOSPHERE A part of the Earth's atmosphere in which the number of ions (electrically charged particles) is enough to affect how radio waves move.

MAGNETOSPHERE A region in the upper atmosphere, or around a planet, where magnetic phenomena such as auroras are found.

PROTONS Positively charged particles from the core of an atom.

SOLAR FLARE Any sudden explosion from the surface of the Sun that sends ultraviolet radiation into the chromosphere. It also sends out some particles that reach Earth and disrupt radio communications.

3: THE SOLAR SYSTEM

The Sun, which has been shining for more than four billion years, is important to the **SOLAR SYSTEM** because it is the prime source of energy of all kinds, including heat, **GRAVITY**, light, **RADIO WAVES**, and **MAGNETISM**. A tiny fraction of this energy reaches the Earth and provides the heat and light that allow life to survive on the planet.

The solar system is made up of a part of space within the **GALAXY** called the **MILKY WAY**.

The vast majority of the solar system is "empty space." Within it, and arranged reasonably evenly, lie small masses of gas and even smaller masses of rock.

The largest mass of gas is a **STAR** we call the Sun. Smaller by far are its dependent **PLANETS**, of which the four gas planets—Jupiter, Saturn, Uranus, and Neptune—are the dominant features. Smaller still are the rocky planets—Mercury, Venus, Earth, Mars, and Pluto. Many of these planets have captive bodies big enough to be called **MOONS**. There are 60 known moons.

Smaller again are the millions of bodies we call **ASTEROIDS** and **COMETS**. There are several thousand asteroids, mostly orbiting between Mars and Jupiter. Beyond Pluto there are several billion small ice and rock bodies that sometimes change direction and move toward Earth. When they do so, they are called comets.

The space between all of these bodies is not quite empty. It consists of occasional particles of ionized (charged) gas called **PLASMA**, with occasional particles of dust. They are mainly particles streaming out from the Sun in the **SOLAR WIND**, as described on page 38.

For more on the planets see Volume 3: *Earth and Moon*, Volume 4: *Rocky planets*, and Volume 5: *Gas giants*.

ASTEROID Any of the many small objects within the solar system.

AXIS (pl. **AXES**) The line around which a body spins.

COMET A small object, often described as being like a dirty snowball, that appears to be very bright in the night sky and has a long tail when it approaches the Sun.

GALAXY A system of stars and interstellar matter within the universe.

GRAVITY The force of attraction between bodies.

MAGNETISM An invisible force that has the property of attracting iron and similar metals.

MILKY WAY The spiral galaxy in which our star and solar system are situated.

MOON The name generally given to any large natural satellite of a planet.

ORBIT The path followed by one object as it tracks around another.

PLANE A flat surface.

PLANET Any of the large bodies that orbit the Sun.

PLASMA A collection of charged particles that behaves something like a gas. It can conduct an electric charge and be affected by magnetic fields.

RADIO WAVES A form of electromagnetic radiation, like light and heat. Radio waves have a longer wavelength than light waves.

SOLAR SYSTEM The Sun and the bodies orbiting around it.

SOLAR WIND The flow of tiny charged particles (called plasma) outward from the Sun.

STAR A large ball of gases that radiates light. The star nearest the Earth is the Sun.

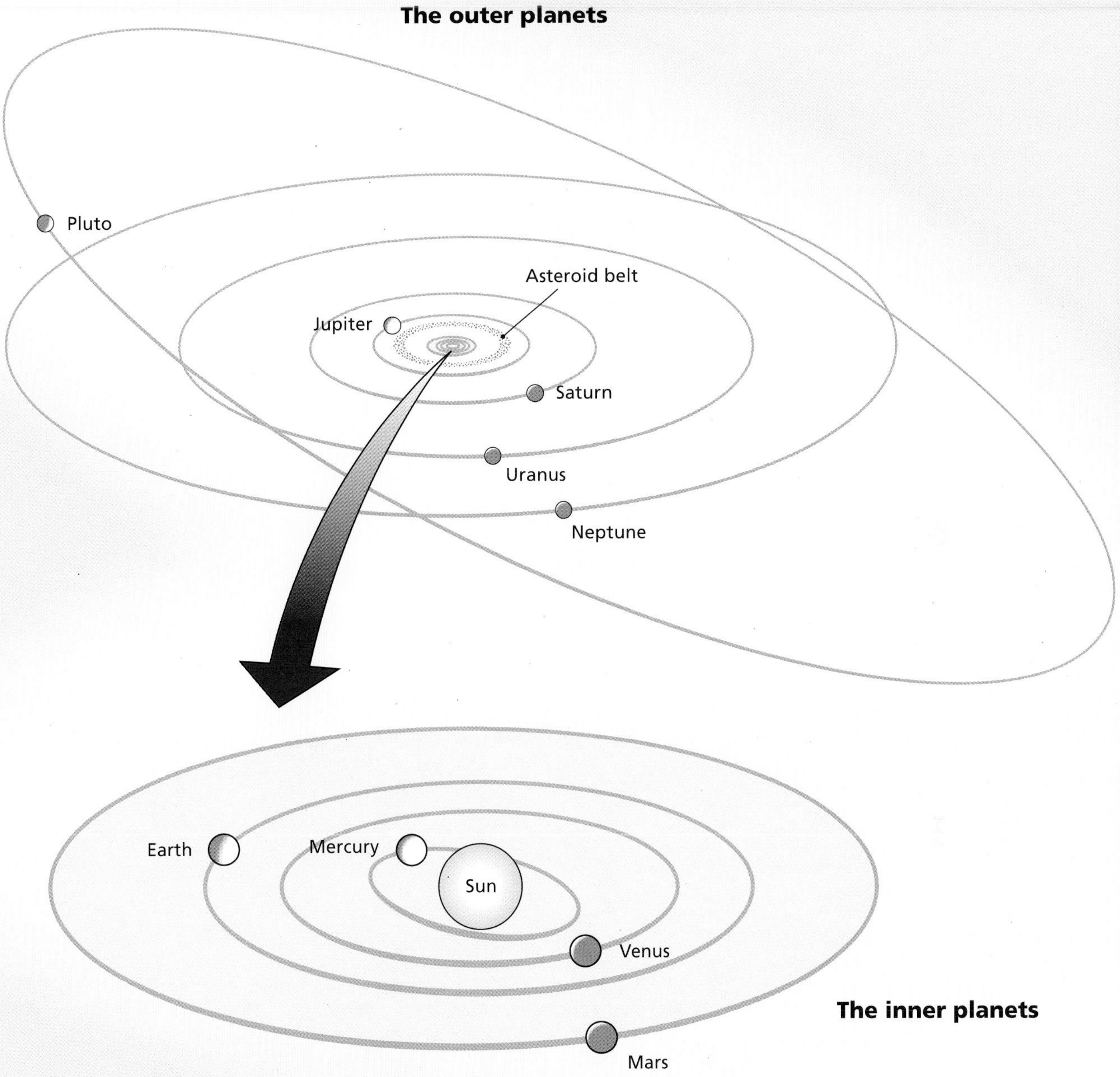

The outer planets

Pluto

Asteroid belt

Jupiter

Saturn

Uranus

Neptune

The inner planets

Earth

Mercury

Sun

Venus

Mars

▲ The Sun and planets all rotate on their AXES. Because they formed from the same spinning disk, the planets, most of their satellites (moons), and the asteroids all revolve around the Sun in the same direction as it turns and in nearly circular ORBITS.

The planets orbit the Sun in, or near, the same PLANE, called the ecliptic (because it is where eclipses occur). Pluto is different in that its orbit is the most highly inclined (17°) and the most highly elliptical (oval) of all the planets.

Organization of the solar system

Although early astronomers believed the Earth to be the center of the universe and that everything rotated around it, we have known since the days of such scientists as Copernicus, Kepler, and Galileo that the Earth is just a small **SATELLITE** of the Sun.

The Earth and the other planets all move in elliptical (oval) paths around the Sun, traveling in a counterclockwise direction. The planets do not all orbit in quite the same plane. That is, if we took a line through the Sun and the Earth, we would find that the orbits of other planets cut across this line. The plane of Pluto's orbit is the most extreme, lying at 17° compared to that of the Earth.

Each planet also spins on an axis that is tilted to the plane of its orbit. These tilts vary, the most extreme being Uranus, which appears to spin lying on its side.

CONDENSE To make something more concentrated or compact.

METEOROID A small body moving in the solar system that becomes a meteor if it enters the Earth's atmosphere.

SATELLITE An object that is in an orbit around another object, usually a planet.

Mars

Venus

Earth

Sun

Mercury

Pluto

Neptune

Uranus

Jupiter

Saturn

▲ The solar system.

The composition of the solar system

Over 99% of the solar system is contained in just one huge ball of gas—our Sun (99.85%).

The other bodies in the solar system are made of a wide collection of different materials. The planets, which **CONDENSED** out of the same disk of material that formed the Sun, contain only about 0.135% of the mass of the solar system, most of it as gas and most of that in Jupiter. Satellites of the planets, comets, asteroids, **METEOROIDS**, and interplanetary medium comprise the remaining 0.015%.

Gas giants

The largest planets are all rotating balls of gas with little or no discernable rocky CORE. They also have very low DENSITIES. (Saturn's density is so low that it would float on water.) They are somewhat similar in composition to the Sun. They also have numerous moons and rings made of small particles of rock that were never captured and incorporated in the planets. Their ATMOSPHERES are mainly hydrogen and helium.

Rocky planets

By contrast, the smaller planets are nearly all made of rock, with only a small mass of gas forming a thin shell.

These planets, apart from Pluto, which seems to be a mixture of rock and ice, have much higher densities than the gas giants. None has rings, and few have moons.

Although all the large bodies in the solar system (including the Sun) have an atmosphere, it is most apparent around the rocky planets because most of the mass of these planets is solid material. The line between the atmosphere and the planet's surface is thus extremely clear-cut, unlike the situation on the gas giants and the Sun.

Although the gases surrounding each rocky planet vary in proportion, they are usually based on oxygen.

Moons

Although we can separate the planets into broad groups, there is great variation among the moons that orbit them. For example, Jupiter's moons are completely different from one another, with the innermost—Io—being one of the most active volcanic places in the solar system, while its neighbor, Europa, is completely devoid of such activity and encased in a skin of ice. Similarly, Saturn's largest moon, Titan, has an atmosphere that is denser than that of the Earth.

For more on Jupiter's moons see Volume 5: *Gas giants*.

Mercury

Venus   Moon

Mars

Earth

Jupiter

Saturn

Uranus

Neptune

Pluto

Comets and asteroids

There is much more uniformity among the **COMETS** and **ASTEROIDS**, suggesting that they are made of materials that more closely resemble the debris from which the planets and moons first formed. That is particularly true of the comets, whose black, sooty ice **NUCLEI** seem never to have changed.

The asteroids and comets travel on very different paths. The asteroids, of which the largest are nearly 1,000 km across, mainly occur between Mars and Jupiter. Some have orbits that occasionally bring them across the orbit of the Earth. In this way there is a very real—if small—danger of collisions between large asteroids and planets like the Earth.

Collisions with small asteroids are quite common. They produce **METEORS** that sometimes burn up in the atmosphere and sometimes crash onto the surface to form features like meteor **CRATERS**. The cratered surfaces of the Moon and many planets testify to the fact that such impacts have been a common experience throughout the history of the solar system.

It is widely believed, for instance, that one large meteor collision was responsible for global climate change and the destruction of the dinosaurs, among other species.

The comets are the most distant things in the solar system. They are grouped beyond Pluto and orbit in various directions, so that they make a shell of sooty bodies at the near edge of the solar system completely invisible to any telescope. There are thought to be two such shells, named the **KUIPER BELT** and the **OORT CLOUD**.

The larger by far is the Oort cloud. Bodies in the Oort cloud may stay in their paths for billions of years. But some get pulled off this stable path, and then they begin to travel across the plane of the planets, developing a **COMA** and a tail that makes them visible even to the naked eye—they become comets.

ASTEROID Any of the many small objects within the solar system.

ATMOSPHERE The envelope of gases that surrounds the Earth and other bodies in the universe.

COMA The blurred image caused by light bouncing from a collection of dust and ice particles escaping from the nucleus of a comet.

COMET A small object, often described as being like a dirty snowball, that appears to be very bright in the night sky and has a long tail when it approaches the Sun.

CORE The central region of a body.

CRATER A deep bowl-shaped depression in the surface of a body formed by the high-speed impact of another, smaller body.

DENSITY A measure of the amount of matter in a space.

KUIPER BELT A belt of planetesimals (small rocky bodies, one kilometer to hundreds of kilometers across) much closer to the Sun than the Oort cloud.

METEOR A streak of light (shooting star) produced by a meteoroid as it enters the Earth's atmosphere.

NUCLEUS (pl. **NUCLEI**) The centermost part of something, the core.

OORT CLOUD A region on the edge of the solar system that consists of planetesimals and comets that did not get caught up in planet making.

For more on comets and asteroids see Volume 4: *Rocky planets*.

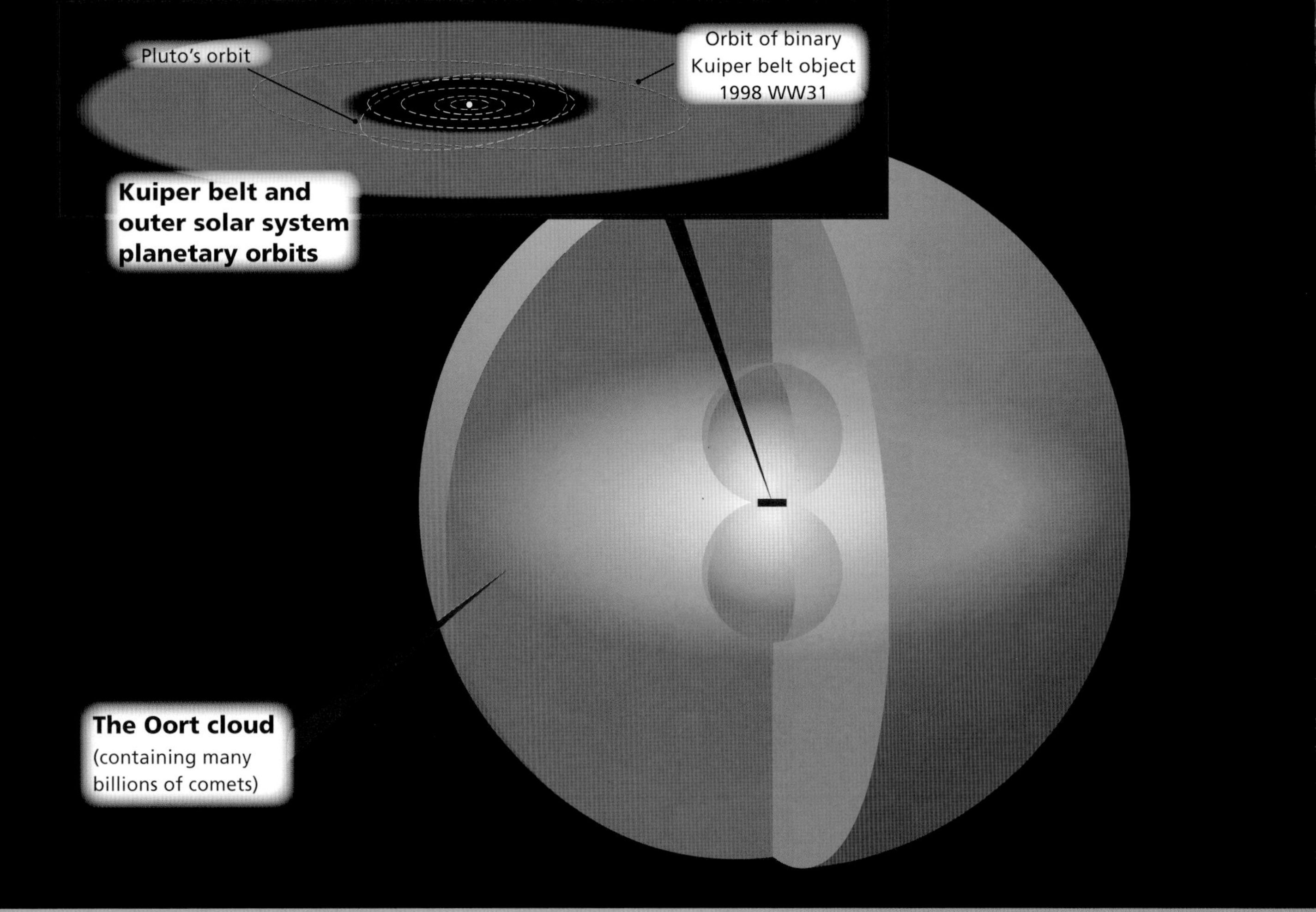

Pluto's orbit

Orbit of binary
Kuiper belt object
1998 WW31

**Kuiper belt and
outer solar system
planetary orbits**

The Oort cloud
(containing many
billions of comets)

▲ The two belts of material that
could make comets: the **OORT
CLOUD** and the **KUIPER BELT**.

Comets give off a constant stream of dust and gas, which
gradually forms a mass of particles that traces out the orbit
of the comet. When the Earth crosses the path of one of these
trails, thousands of small dust particles enter the atmosphere
and burn up, creating a meteor shower.

How the solar system was formed

Finding out about the origin of the solar system is one of
the biggest challenges facing astronomers. Although our
knowledge of space has increased immeasurably over the last
few decades as space **PROBES** have sent back much invaluable
information, we are still only scratching the surface.

We can begin to find out about how the solar system
formed by analyzing the materials that reach the Earth from
space in the form of **METEORITES**.

The amount of this material that gets to Earth is surprisingly large. Every day 400 tonnes of dust are added to the mass of the Earth by debris from asteroids and comets. You can start to see a way in which planets could grow when you consider the billions of years of Earth history. In the past, when there was much more material in space, the rate of growth would have been much faster.

Models of the origin of the solar system

The first description of how the solar system works was made possible using the LAWS OF MOTION set out by Sir Isaac Newton in 1687. They explained how GRAVITY affected bodies as well as why planets should orbit the Sun. Gravity is the force that draws space debris together and creates not just rocky planets like the Earth but gaseous planets and even the Sun.

A scientifically reasoned explanation of the origin of the solar system was first suggested by Immanuel Kant in 1755. He believed that the solar system started as a cloud of dust, and that gravity then made the dust particles move. As they did so, they collided and formed larger and larger bodies. Those that grew faster developed stronger gravity and began to attract more and more dust, thus growing faster still.

Pierre-Simon Laplace suggested that the planets were made from a gigantic star, or NEBULA, with an atmosphere (called the CORONA) stretching to the edges of the solar system. He thought that the star had cooled through time and so shrunk. The shrinking would have made it spin faster (as ice-skaters do when they spin and pull in their arms). That would tend to throw some material away from the star; but at the same time, most of it would be pulled inward by gravity. The result of these conflicting forces would be the creation of a disk of material. The planets would have formed in this disk.

This model explained why the Sun and the planets all move in more or less the same plane and in the same direction.

By the early 20th century Chrowder Chamberlin, Forest Ray Moulton, Sir James Jeans, and Sir Harold Jeffreys all decided independently that the planets were formed by the collision resulting from our Sun sweeping very close to another star. The intense gravity would pull material away from the stars and form a disk, which would later begin to form into planets. But observations show that near-star events are very rare.

CORONA (pl. CORONAE) The gases surrounding a star such as the Sun. In the case of the Sun and certain other stars these gases are extremely hot.

GRAVITY The force of attraction between bodies.

KUIPER BELT A belt of planetesimals (small rocky bodies, one kilometer to hundreds of kilometers across) much closer to the Sun than the Oort cloud.

LAWS OF MOTION Formulated by Sir Isaac Newton, they describe the forces that act on a moving object.

METEORITE A meteor that reaches the Earth's surface.

NEBULA (pl. NEBULAE) Clouds of gas and dust that exist in the space between stars.

OORT CLOUD A region on the edge of the solar system that consists of planetesimals and comets that did not get caught up in planet making.

PROBE An unmanned spacecraft designed to explore our solar system and beyond.

For explanations of how galaxies and the universe may have formed see Volume 1: *How the universe works*.

Modern ideas

Many of these early ideas were based on the belief that stars contained solid materials. But then it was discovered that they are, in fact, balls of gas. So some means of getting the material to **CONDENSE** into planets was then required.

Moreover, it became clear that stars (including the Sun) form inside clouds of gas and dust rather than create them. So, scientists began to look for a way that the planets and the stars could have been made at the same time.

Today, many scientists think that the solar system began as a cloud of gas and dust (a **SUPERNOVA**) that started to collapse inward on itself as it moved through a spiral arm of the galaxy.

As this happened, the cloud became denser. Because the gravity of the galaxy would affect the cloud differently on the side nearest the center of the galaxy than on the side away from it, gravity would start to make the collapsing cloud rotate. At the same time, it would flatten into a disk. This is called the solar **NEBULA**. It would have looked like a tiny galaxy with spiral arms containing more concentrated regions of dust and gas.

As the dust and gas were pulled to the center of the nebula, they spun faster and heated up. At the center of this spiral speeds and temperatures got great enough for nuclear reactions to take place and so create a star, in this case our Sun.

At the same time, planets began to grow in the outer arms of the spirals, much as Kant had originally suggested. The planets then began to influence one another, possibly changing their orbits as a result. Some early planets probably collided, shedding the particles that we now partly see as the asteroids. Some collisions may have been catastrophic but not fatal, for example, causing Uranus to turn onto its side, and possibly making a great chunk of the Earth break away and form the Moon.

CONDENSE To make something more concentrated or compact.

FALSE COLOR The colors used to make the appearance of some property more obvious.

NEBULA (pl. **NEBULAE**) Clouds of gas and dust that exist in the space between stars.

SUPERNOVA A violently exploding star that becomes millions or even billions of times brighter than when it was younger and stable.

▲ This is a collection, or montage, of the nine planets and four large moons of Jupiter set against a **FALSE-COLOR** view of the Rosette Nebula.

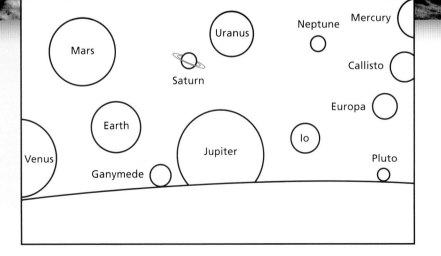

Mars

Uranus

Neptune

Mercury

Saturn

Callisto

Europa

Earth

Io

Venus

Jupiter

Pluto

Ganymede

▲ A **NEBULA** like the one that might have been the birthplace of the solar system.

Why there are rocky and gas planets

So, how did we end up with some planets of rock, others of gas, and an awful lot of water (mostly as ice) around? To answer this, we need to look to see what space is made of. Space is made up of **ATOMS** of **ELEMENTS** such as silicon, hydrogen, oxygen, and helium. Silicon, hydrogen, and oxygen can combine in various ways to make **MOLECULES**.

Helium is unreactive. Hydrogen and oxygen are very reactive. Silicon and oxygen combine to form silica (rock), and oxygen and hydrogen combine to form water. But in space there are 24 oxygen atoms for every silicon atom. So, after a while all of the silicon atoms would have reacted. That limits the amount of rock that can form. There are a thousand hydrogen atoms for every oxygen atom. The reaction of these two elements makes water the most common molecule in the universe but still leaves an immense amount of hydrogen that has not reacted.

ATOM The smallest particle of an element.

ELEMENT A substance that cannot be decomposed into simpler substances by chemical means.

GRAVITY The force of attraction between bodies.

INNER PLANETS The rocky planets closest to the Sun. They are Mercury, Venus, Earth, and Mars.

MOLECULE A group of two or more atoms held together by chemical bonds.

MOLTEN Liquid, suggesting that it has changed from a solid.

NEBULA (pl. **NEBULAE**) Clouds of gas and dust that exist in the space between stars.

OUTER PLANETS The gas giant planets Jupiter, Saturn, Uranus, and Neptune plus the rocky planet Pluto.

Close to the Sun it is too hot for water to freeze, but from Jupiter outward it is too cold for it to stay liquid. So, objects in the cool regions of the solar system have much more material to build with (that is, they have rock and water) than those close to the Sun (which have only rock).

As planets grow, their **GRAVITY** becomes stronger. When they are ten times the mass of the Earth, they have a sufficiently powerful gravity to attract helium and hydrogen atoms, and so they can continue to grow using the most plentiful material left in space. That allows ice-cored gas planets to become more and more massive—surrounded by hydrogen and helium.

In the outer regions of the solar system the planets grew to such a size that they attracted material from around them, which then formed a disk like a miniature solar system. It is the material from which the present rings of the giant planets were formed.

Planets like Jupiter would also have been so hot as they grew to full size that ice could not freeze close to them. As a result, the kinds of moons found away from the giant planets change, just as the nature of the planets changes away from the Sun. In the case of Jupiter the inner moons are rocky and have a high density, while the outer ones have a much lower density.

This explanation suggests why the **INNER PLANETS** are rocky and of high density and have matching moons, while the **OUTER PLANETS** have a lower density and have some high-density moons and some low-density moons.

A timeline for the solar system

How long would all of this take? Present estimates suggest that the planets formed in a very short time. A body 10 kilometers across could form in a thousand years, a planet in 10 million years.

As these bodies grew, they became hotter, and many developed **MOLTEN** cores.

After this astonishingly rapid growth the material in the solar system was largely used up, so that growth slowed. Nevertheless, it is still occurring today as the crashing of meteorites on the Earth's surface shows.

SET GLOSSARY

ABSOLUTE ZERO The coldest possible temperature, defined as 0 K or –273°C.
See also: **K**.

ACCELERATE To gain speed.

AERODYNAMIC A shape offering as little resistance to the air as possible.

AIR RESISTANCE The frictional drag that an object creates as it moves rapidly through the air.

AMINO ACIDS Simple organic molecules that can be building blocks for living things.

ANNULAR Ringlike.
An annular eclipse occurs when the dark disk of the Moon does not completely obscure the Sun.

ANTENNA (pl. **ANTENNAE**) A device, often in the shape of a rod or wire, used for sending out and receiving radio waves.

ANTICLINE An arching fold of rock layers where the rocks slope down from the crest.

ANTICYCLONE A roughly circular region of the atmosphere that is spiraling outward and downward.

APOGEE The point on an orbit where the orbiting object is at its farthest from the object it is orbiting.

APOLLO The program developed in the United States by NASA to get people to the Moon's surface and back safely.

ARRAY A regular group or arrangement.

ASH Fragments of lava that have cooled and solidified between when they leave a volcano and when they fall to the surface.

ASTEROID Any of the many small objects within the solar system.
Asteroids are rocky or metallic and are conventionally described as significant bodies with a diameter smaller than 1,000 km. Asteroids mainly occupy a belt between Mars and Jupiter (asteroid belt).

ASTEROID BELT The collection of asteroids that orbit the Sun between the orbits of Mars and Jupiter.

ASTHENOSPHERE The region below the lithosphere, and therefore part of the upper mantle, in which some material may be molten.

ASTRONOMICAL UNIT (**AU**) The average distance from the Earth to the Sun (149,597,870 km).

ASTRONOMY The study of space beyond the Earth and its contents. It includes those phenomena that affect the Earth but that originate in space, such as meteorites and aurora.

ASTROPHYSICS The study of physics in space, what other stars, galaxies, and planets are like, and the physical laws that govern them.

ASYNCHRONOUS Not connected in time or pace.

ATMOSPHERE The envelope of gases that surrounds the Earth and other bodies in the universe.
The Earth's atmosphere is very different from that of other planets, being, for example, far lower in hydrogen and helium than the gas giants and lower in carbon dioxide than Venus, but richer in oxygen than all the others.

ATMOSPHERIC PRESSURE The pressure on the gases in the atmosphere caused by gravity pulling them toward the center of a celestial body.

ATOM The smallest particle of an element.

ATOMIC MASS UNIT A measure of the mass of an atom or molecule.
An atomic mass unit equals one-twelfth of the mass of an atom of carbon-12.

ATOMIC WEAPONS Weapons that rely on the violent explosive force achieved when radioactive materials are made to go into an uncontrollable chain reaction.

ATOMIC WEIGHT The ratio of the average mass of a chemical element's atoms to carbon-12.

AURORA A region of illumination, often in the form of a wavy curtain, high in the atmosphere of a planet.
It is the result of the interaction of the planet's magnetic field with the particles in the solar wind. High-energy electrons from the solar wind race along the planet's magnetic field into the upper atmosphere. The electrons excite atmospheric gases, making them glow.

AXIS (pl. **AXES**) The line around which a body spins.
The Earth spins around an axis through its north and south geographic poles.

BALLISTIC MISSILE A rocket that is guided up in a high arching path; then the fuel supply is cut, and it is allowed to fall to the ground.

BASIN A large depression in the ground (bigger than a crater).

BIG BANG The theory that the universe as we know it started from a single point (called a singularity) and then exploded outward. It is still expanding today.

BINARY STAR A pair of stars that are gravitationally attracted, and that revolve around one another.

BLACK DWARF A degenerate star that has cooled so that it is now not visible.

BLACK HOLE An object that has a gravitational pull so strong that nothing can escape from it.
A black hole may have a mass equal to thousands of stars or more.

BLUE GIANT A young, extremely bright and hot star of very large mass that has used up all its hydrogen and is no longer in the main sequence. When a blue giant ages, it becomes a red giant.

BOILING POINT The change of state of a substance in which a liquid rapidly turns into a gas without a change in temperature.

BOOSTER POD A form of housing that stands outside the main body of the launcher.

CALDERA A large pit in the top of a volcano produced when the top of the volcano explodes and collapses in on itself.

CAPSULE A small pressurized space vehicle.

CATALYST A substance that speeds up a chemical reaction but that is itself unchanged.

CELESTIAL Relating to the sky above, the "heavens."

CENTER OF GRAVITY The point at which all of the mass of an object can be balanced.

CENTRIFUGAL FORCE A force that acts on an orbiting or spinning body, tending to oppose gravity and move away from the center of rotation.
For orbiting objects the centrifugal force acts in the opposite direction from gravity. When satellites orbit the Earth, the centrifugal force balances out the force of gravity.

CENTRIFUGE An instrument for spinning small samples very rapidly.

CHAIN REACTION A sequence of related events with one event triggering the next.

CHASM A deep, narrow trench.

CHROMOSPHERE The shell of gases that makes up part of the atmosphere of a star and lies between the photosphere and the corona.

CIRCUMFERENCE The distance around the edge of a circle or sphere.

COMA The blurred image caused by light bouncing from a collection of dust and ice particles escaping from the nucleus of a comet.

The coma changes the appearance of a comet from a point source of reflective light to a blurry object with a tail.

COMBUSTION CHAMBER A vessel inside an engine or motor where the fuel components mix and are set on fire, that is, they are burned (combusted).

COMET A small object, often described as being like a dirty snowball, that appears to be very bright in the night sky and has a long tail when it approaches the Sun.

Comets are thought to be some of the oldest objects in the solar system.

COMPLEMENTARY COLOR A color that is diametrically opposed in the range, or circle, of colors in the spectrum; for example, cyan (blue) is the complement of red.

COMPOSITE A material made from solid threads in a liquid matrix that is allowed to set.

COMPOUND A substance made from two or more elements that have chemically combined.

Ammonia is an example of a compound made from the elements hydrogen and nitrogen.

CONDENSE/CONDENSATION (1) To make something more concentrated or compact.

(2) The change of state from a gas or vapor to a liquid.

CONDUCTION The transfer of heat between two objects when they touch.

CONSTELLATION One of many commonly recognized patterns of stars in the sky.

CONVECTION/CONVECTION CURRENTS The circulating flow in a fluid (liquid or gas) that occurs when it is heated from below.

Convective flow is caused in a fluid by the tendency for hotter, and therefore less dense, material to rise and for colder, and therefore more dense, material, to sink with gravity. That results in a heat transfer.

CORE The central region of a body.

The core of the Earth is about 3,300 km in radius, compared with the radius of the whole Earth, which is 6,300 km.

CORONA (pl. **CORONAE**) (1) A colored circle seen around a bright object such as a star.

(2) The gases surrounding a star such as the Sun. In the case of the Sun and certain other stars these gases are extremely hot.

(3) A circular to oval pattern of faults, fractures, and ridges with a sagging center as found on Venus. In the case of Venus they are a few hundred kilometers in diameter.

CORONAL MASS EJECTIONS Very large bubbles of plasma escaping into the corona.

CORROSIVE SUBSTANCE Something that chemically eats away something else.

COSMOLOGICAL PRINCIPLE States that the way you see the universe is independent of the place where you are (your location). In effect, it means that the universe is roughly uniform throughout.

COSMONAUT A Russian space person.

COSMOS The universe and everything in it. The word "cosmos" suggests that the universe operates according to orderly principles.

CRATER A deep bowl-shaped depression in the surface of a body formed by the high-speed impact of another, smaller body.

Most craters are formed by the impact of asteroids and meteoroids. Craters have both a depression, or pit, and also an elevated rim formed of the material displaced from the central pit.

CRESCENT The appearance of the Moon when it is between a new Moon and a half Moon.

CRUST The solid outer surface of a rocky body.

The crust of the Earth is mainly just a few tens of kilometers thick, compared to the total radius of 6,300 km for the whole Earth. It forms much of the lithosphere.

CRYSTAL An ordered arrangement of molecules in a compound. Crystals that grow freely develop flat surfaces.

CYCLONE A large storm in which the atmosphere spirals inward and upward.

On Earth cyclones have a very low atmospheric pressure at their center and often contain deep clouds.

DARK MATTER Matter that does not shine or reflect light.

No one has ever found dark matter, but it is thought to exist because the amount of ordinary matter in the universe is not enough to account for many gravitational effects that have been observed.

DENSITY A measure of the amount of matter in a space.

Density is often measured in grams per cubic centimeter. The density of the Earth is 5.5 grams per cubic centimeter.

DEORBIT To move out of an orbital position and begin a reentry path toward the Earth.

DEPRESSION (1) A sunken area or hollow in a surface or landscape.

(2) A region of inward swirling air in the atmosphere associated with cloudy weather and rain.

DIFFRACTION The bending of light as it goes through materials of different density.

DISK A shape or surface that looks round and flat.

DOCK To meet with and attach to another space vehicle.

DOCKING PORT/STATION A place on the side of a spacecraft that contains some form of anchoring mechanism and an airlock.

DOPPLER EFFECT The apparent change in pitch of a fast-moving object as it approaches or leaves an observer.

DOWNLINK A communication to Earth from a spacecraft.

DRAG A force that hinders the movement of something.

DWARF STAR A star that shines with a brightness that is average or below.

EARTH The third planet from the Sun and the one on which we live.

The Earth belongs to the group of rocky planets. It is unique in having an oxygen-rich atmosphere and water, commonly found in its three phases—solid, liquid, and gas.

EARTHQUAKE The shock waves produced by the sudden movement of two pieces of brittle crust.

ECCENTRIC A noncircular, or oval, orbit.

ECLIPSE The time when light is cut off by a body coming between the observer and the source of the illumination (for example, eclipse of the Sun), or when the body the observer is on comes between the source of illumination and another body (for example, eclipse of the Moon).

It happens when three bodies are in a line. This phenomenon is not necessarily called an eclipse. Occultations of stars by the Moon and transits of Venus or Mercury are examples of different expressions used instead of "eclipse."

See also: **TOTAL ECLIPSE.**

ECOLOGY The study of living things in their environment.

ELECTRONS Negatively charged particles that are parts of atoms.

ELEMENT A substance that cannot be decomposed into simpler substances by chemical means.

Elements are the building blocks of compounds. For example, silicon and oxygen are elements. They combine to form the compound silicon dioxide, or quartz.

ELLIPTICAL GALAXY A galaxy that has an oval shape rather like a football, and that has no spiral arms.

EL NIÑO A time when ocean currents in the Pacific Ocean reverse from their normal pattern and disrupt global weather patterns. It occurs once every 4 or 5 years.

EMISSION Something that is sent or let out.

ENCKE GAP A gap between rings around Saturn named for the astronomer Johann Franz Encke (1791–1865).

EPOXY RESIN Adhesives that develop their strength as they react, or "cure," after mixing.

EQUATOR The ring drawn around a body midway between the poles.

EQUILIBRIUM A state of balance.

ESA The European Space Agency. ESA is an organizaton of European countries for cooperation in space research and technology. It operates several installations around Europe and has its headquarters in Paris, France.

ESCARPMENT A sharp-edged ridge.

EVAPORATE/EVAPORATION The change in state from liquid to a gas.

EXOSPHERE The outer part of the atmosphere starting about 500 km from the surface. This layer contains so little air that molecules rarely collide.

EXTRAVEHICULAR ACTIVITY Any task performed by people outside the protected environment of a space vehicle's pressurized compartments. Extravehicular activities (EVA) include repairing equipment in the Space Shuttle bay.

FALSE COLOR The colors used to make the appearance of some property more obvious.
They are part of the computer generation of an image.

FAULT A place in the crust where rocks have fractured, and then one side has moved relative to the other.
A fault is caused by excessive pressure on brittle rocks.

FLUORESCENT Emitting the visible light produced by a substance when it is struck by invisible waves, such as ultraviolet waves.

FRACTURE A break in brittle rock.

FREQUENCY The number of complete cycles of (for example, radio) waves received per second.

FRICTION The force that resists two bodies that are in contact.
For example, the effect of the ocean waters moving as tides slows the Earth's rotation.

FUSION The joining of atomic nuclei to form heavier nuclei.
This process results in the release of huge amounts of energy.

GALAXY A system of stars and interstellar matter within the universe.
Galaxies may contain billions of stars.

GALILEAN SATELLITES The four large satellites of Jupiter discovered by astronomer Galileo Galilei in 1610. They are Callisto, Europa, Ganymede, and Io.

GALILEO A U.S. space probe launched in October 1989 and designed for intensive investigation of Jupiter.

GEIGER TUBE A device to detect radioactive materials.

GEOSTATIONARY ORBIT A circular orbit 35,786 km directly above the Earth's equator.
Communications satellites frequently use this orbit. A satellite in a geostationary orbit will move at the same rate as the Earth's rotation, completing one revolution in 24 hours. That way it remains at the same point over the Earth's equator.

GEOSTATIONARY SATELLITE A man-made satellite in a fixed or geosynchronous orbit around the Earth.

GEOSYNCHRONOUS ORBIT An orbit in which a satellite makes one circuit of the Earth in 24 hours.
A geosynchronous orbit coincides with the Earth's orbit—it takes the same time to

complete an orbit as it does for the Earth to make one complete rotation. If the orbit is circular and above the equator, then the satellite remains over one particular point of the equator; that is called a geostationary orbit.

GEOSYNCLINE A large downward sag or trench that forms in the Earth's crust as a result of colliding tectonic plates.

GEYSER A periodic fountain of material. On Earth geysers are of water and steam, but on other planets and moons they are formed from other substances, for example, nitrogen gas on Triton.

GIBBOUS When between half and a full disk of a body can be seen lighted by the Sun.

GIMBALS A framework that allows anything inside it to move in a variety of directions.

GLOBAL POSITIONING SYSTEM A network of geostationary satellites that can be used to locate the position of any object on the Earth's surface.

GRANULATION The speckled pattern we see in the Sun's photosphere as a result of convectional overturning of gases.

GRAVITATIONAL FIELD The region surrounding a body in which that body's gravitational force can be felt.
The gravitational field of the Sun spreads over the entire solar system. The gravitational fields of the planets each exert some influence on the orbits of their neighbors.

GRAVITY/GRAVITATIONAL FORCE/ GRAVITATIONAL PULL The force of attraction between bodies. The larger an object, the more its gravitational pull on other objects.
The Sun's gravity is the most powerful in the solar system, keeping all of the planets and other materials within the solar system.

GREAT RED SPOT A large, almost permanent feature of the Jovian atmosphere that moves around the planet at about latitude 23°S.

GREENHOUSE EFFECT The increase in atmospheric temperature produced by the presence of carbon dioxide in the air.
Carbon dioxide has the ability to soak up heat radiated from the surface of a planet and partly prevent its escape. The effect is similar to that produced by a greenhouse.

GROUND STATION A receiving and transmitting station in direct communication with satellites. Such stations are characterized by having large dish-shaped antennae.

GULLY (pl. **GULLIES**) A trench in the land surface formed, on Earth, by running water.

GYROSCOPE A device in which a rapidly spinning wheel is held in a frame in such a way that it can rotate in any direction. The momentum of the wheel means that the gyroscope retains its position even when the frame is tilted.

HEAT SHIELD A protective device on the outside of a space vehicle that absorbs the heat during reentry and protects it from burning up.

HELIOPAUSE The edge of the heliosphere.

HELIOSEISMOLOGY The study of the internal structure of the Sun by modeling the Sun's patterns of internal shock waves.

HELIOSPHERE The entire range of influence of the Sun. It extends to the edge of the solar system.

HUBBLE SPACE TELESCOPE An orbiting telescope (and so a satellite) that was placed above the Earth's atmosphere so that it could take images that were far clearer than anything that could be obtained from the surface of the Earth.

HURRICANE A very violent cyclone that begins close to the equator, and that contains winds of over 117 km/hr.

ICE CAP A small mountainous region that is covered in ice.

INFRARED Radiation with a wavelength that is longer than red light.

INNER PLANETS The rocky planets closest to the Sun. They are Mercury, Venus, Earth, and Mars.

INTERNATIONAL SPACE STATION The international orbiting space laboratory.

INTERPLANETARY DUST The fine dustlike material that lies scattered through space, and that exists between the planets as well as in outer space.

INTERSTELLAR Between the stars.

IONIZED Matter that has been converted into small charged particles called ions.
An atom that has gained or lost an electron.

IONOSPHERE A part of the Earth's atmosphere in which the number of ions (electrically charged particles) is enough to affect how radio waves move.
The ionosphere begins about 50 km above the Earth's surface.

IRREGULAR SATELLITES Satellites that orbit in the opposite direction from their parent planet.
This motion is also called retrograde rotation.

ISOTOPE Atoms that have the same number of protons in their nucleus, but that have different masses; for example, carbon-12 and carbon-14.

JOVIAN PLANETS An alternative group name for the gas giant planets: Jupiter, Saturn, Uranus, and Neptune.

JUPITER The fifth planet from the Sun and two planets farther away from the Sun than the Earth.
Jupiter is 318 times as massive as the Earth and 1,500 times as big by volume. It is the largest of the gas giants.

K Named for British scientist Lord Kelvin (1824–1907), it is a measurement of absolute temperature. Zero K is called absolute zero and is only approached in deep space: ice melts at 273 K, and water boils at 373 K.

KEELER GAP A gap in the rings of Saturn named for the astronomer James Edward Keeler (1857–1900).

KILOPARSEC A unit of a thousand parsecs. A parsec is the unit used for measuring the largest distances in the universe.

KUIPER BELT A belt of planetesimals (small rocky bodies, one kilometer to hundreds of kilometers across) much closer to the Sun than the Oort cloud.

LANDSLIDE A sudden collapse of material on a steep slope.

LA NIÑA Below normal ocean temperatures in the eastern Pacific Ocean that disrupt global weather patterns.

LATITUDE Angular distance north or south of the equator, measured through 90°.

LAUNCH VEHICLE/LAUNCHER A system of propellant tanks and rocket motors or engines designed to lift a payload into space. It may, or may not, be part of a space vehicle.

LAVA Hot, melted rock from a volcano.

Lava flows onto the surface of a planet and cools and hardens to form new rock. Most of the lava on Earth is made of basalt.

LAVA FLOW A river or sheet of liquid volcanic rock.

LAWS OF MOTION Formulated by Sir Isaac Newton, they describe the forces that act on a moving object.

The first law states that an object will keep moving in a straight line at constant speed unless it is acted on by a force.

The second law states that the force on an object is related to the mass of the object multiplied by its acceleration.

The third law states that an action always has an equal and directly opposite reaction.

LIFT An upthrust on the wing of a plane that occurs when it moves rapidly through the air. It is the main way of suspending an airplane during flight. The engines simply provide the forward thrust.

LIGHT-YEAR The distance traveled by light through space in one Earth year, or 63,240 astronomical units.

The speed of light is the speed that light travels through a vacuum, which is 299,792 km/s.

LIMB The outer edge of a celestial body, including an atmosphere if it has one.

LITHOSPHERE The upper part of the Earth, corresponding generally to the crust and believed to be about 80 km thick.

LOCAL GROUP The Milky Way, the Magellanic Clouds, the Andromeda Galaxy, and over 20 other relatively near galaxies.

LUNAR Anything to do with the Moon.

MAGELLANIC CLOUD Either of two small galaxies that are companions to the Milky Way Galaxy.

MAGMA Hot, melted rock inside the Earth that, when cooled, forms igneous rock.

Magma is associated with volcanic activity.

MAGNETIC FIELD The region of influence of a magnetic body.

The Earth's magnetic field stretches out beyond the atmosphere into space. There it interacts with the solar wind to produce auroras.

MAGNETISM An invisible force that has the property of attracting iron and similar metals.

MAGNETOPAUSE The outer edge of the magnetosphere.

MAGNETOSPHERE A region in the upper atmosphere, or around a planet, where magnetic phenomena such as auroras are found.

MAGNITUDE A measure of the brightness of a star.

The apparent magnitude is the brightness of a celestial object as seen from the Earth. The absolute magnitude is the standardized brightness measured as though all objects were the same distance from the Earth. The brighter the object, the lower its magnitude number. For example, a star of magnitude 4 is 2.5 times as bright as one of magnitude 5. A difference of five magnitudes is the same as a difference in brightness of 100 to 1. The brightest stars have negative numbers. The Sun's apparent magnitude is −26.8. Its absolute magnitude is 4.8.

MAIN SEQUENCE The 90% of stars in the universe that represent the mature phase of stars with small or medium mass.

MANTLE The region of a planet between the core and the crust.

The Earth's mantle is about 2,900 km thick, and its upper surface may be molten in some places.

MARE (pl. **MARIA**) A flat, dark plain created by lava flows. They were once thought to be seas.

MARS The fourth planet from the Sun in our solar system and one planet farther away from the Sun than the Earth.

Mars is a rocky planet almost half the diameter of Earth that is a distinctive rust-red color.

MASCON A region of higher surface density on the Moon.

MASS The amount of matter in an object.

The amount of matter, and so the mass, remains the same, but the effect of gravity gives the mass a weight. The weight depends on the gravitational pull. Thus a ball will have the same mass on the Earth and on the Moon, but it will weigh a sixth as much on the Moon because the force of gravity there is only a sixth as strong.

MATTER Anything that exists in physical form.

Everything we can see is made of matter. The building blocks of matter are atoms.

MERCURY The closest planet to the Sun in our solar system and two planets closer to the Sun than Earth.

Mercury is a gray-colored rocky planet less than half the diameter of Earth. It has the most extreme temperature range of any planet in our solar system.

MESOSPHERE One of the upper regions of the atmosphere, beginning at the top of the stratosphere and continuing from 50 km upward until the temperature stops declining.

METEOR A streak of light (shooting star) produced by a meteoroid as it enters the Earth's atmosphere.

The friction with the Earth's atmosphere causes the small body to glow (become incandescent). That is what we see as a streak of light.

METEORITE A meteor that reaches the Earth's surface.

METEOROID A small body moving in the solar system that becomes a meteor if it enters the Earth's atmosphere.

Meteoroids are typically only a few millimeters across and burn up as they go through the atmosphere, but some have crashed to the Earth, making large craters.

MICROMETEORITES Tiny pieces of space dust moving at high speeds.

MICRON A millionth of a meter.

MICROWAVELENGTH Waves at the shortest end of the radio wavelengths.

MICROWAVE RADIATION The background radiation that is found everywhere in space, and whose existence is used to support the Big Bang theory.

MILKY WAY The spiral galaxy in which our star and solar system are situated.

MINERAL A solid crystalline substance.

MINOR PLANET Another term for an asteroid.

M NUMBER In 1781 Charles Messier began a catalogue of the objects he could see in the night sky. He gave each of them a unique number. The first entry was called M1. There is no significance to the number in terms of brightness, size, closeness, or otherwise.

MODULE A section, or part, of a space vehicle.

MOLECULE A group of two or more atoms held together by chemical bonds.

MOLTEN Liquid, suggesting that it has changed from a solid.

MOMENTUM The mass of an object multiplied by its velocity.

MOON The natural satellite that orbits the Earth.

Other planets have large satellites, or moons, but none is relatively as large as our Moon, suggesting that it has a unique origin.

MOON The name generally given to any large natural satellite of a planet.

MOUNTAIN RANGE A long, narrow region of very high land that contains several or many mountains.

NASA The National Aeronautics and Space Administration.

NASA was founded in 1958 for aeronautical and space exploration. It operates several installations around the country and has its headquarters in Washington, D.C.

NEAP TIDE A tide showing the smallest difference between high and low tides.

NEBULA (pl. **NEBULAE**) Clouds of gas and dust that exist in the space between stars.

The word means mist or cloud and is also used as an alternative to galaxy. The gas makes up to 5% of the mass of a galaxy. What a nebula looks like depends on the arrangement of gas and dust within it.

NEPTUNE The eighth planet from the Sun in our solar system and five planets farther away from the Sun than the Earth.

Neptune is a gas planet that is almost four times the diameter of Earth. It is blue.

NEUTRINOS An uncharged fundamental particle that is thought to have no mass.

NEUTRONS Particles inside the core of an atom that are neutral (have no charge).

NEUTRON STAR A very dense star that consists only of tightly packed neutrons. It is the result of the collapse of a massive star.

NOBLE GASES The unreactive gases, such as neon, xenon, and krypton.

NOVA (pl. **NOVAE**) (1) A star that suddenly becomes much brighter, then fades away to its original brightness within a few months.
See also: **SUPERNOVA**.

(2) A radiating pattern of faults and fractures unique to Venus.

NUCLEAR DEVICES Anything that is powered by a source of radioactivity.

NUCLEUS (pl. **NUCLEI**) The centermost part of something, the core.

OORT CLOUD A region on the edge of the solar system that consists of planetesimals and comets that did not get caught up in planet making.

OPTICAL Relating to the use of light.

ORBIT The path followed by one object as it tracks around another.

The orbits of the planets around the Sun and moons around their planets are oval, or elliptical.

ORGANIC MATERIAL Any matter that contains carbon and is alive.

OUTER PLANETS The gas giant planets Jupiter, Saturn, Uranus, and Neptune plus the rocky planet Pluto.

OXIDIZER The substance in a reaction that removes electrons from and thereby oxidizes (burns) another substance.

In the case of oxygen this results in the other substance combining with the oxygen to form an oxide (also called an oxidizing agent).

OZONE A form of oxygen (O_3) with three atoms in each molecule instead of the more usual two (O_2).

OZONE HOLE The observed lack of the gas ozone in the upper atmosphere.

PARSEC The unit used for measuring the largest distances in the universe.

A parsec is the distance at which an observer in space would see the radius of the orbit as making one second of arc. This gives a distance of about 3.26 light-years.
See also: **KILOPARSEC**.

PAYLOAD The spacecraft that is carried into space by a launcher.

PENUMBRA (1) A region that is in semidarkness during an eclipse.

(2) The part of a sunspot surrounding the umbra.

PERCOLATE To flow by gravity between particles, for example, of soil.

PERIGEE The point on an orbit where the orbiting object is as close as it ever comes to the object it is orbiting.

PHARMACEUTICAL Relating to medicinal drugs.

PHASE The differing appearance of a body that is closer to the Sun, and that is illuminated by it.

PHOTOCHEMICAL SMOG A hazy atmosphere, often brown, resulting from the reaction of nitrogen gases with sunlight.

PHOTOMOSAIC A composite picture made up of several other pictures that individually only cover a small area.

PHOTON A particle (quantum) of electromagnetic radiation.

PHOTOSPHERE A shell of the Sun that we regard as its visible surface.

PHOTOSYNTHESIS The process that plants use to combine the substances in the environment, such as carbon dioxide, minerals, and water, with oxygen and energy-rich organic compounds by using the energy of sunlight.

PIONEER A name for a series of unmanned U.S. spacecraft.

Pioneer 1 was launched into lunar orbit on October 11, 1958. The others all went into deep space.

PLAIN A flat or gently rolling part of a landscape.

Plains are confined to lowlands. If a flat surface exists in an upland, it is called a plateau.

PLANE A flat surface.

PLANET Any of the large bodies that orbit the Sun.

The planets are (outward from the Sun): Mercury, Venus, Earth, Mars, Jupiter, Saturn, Uranus, Neptune, and Pluto. The rocky planets all have densities greater than 3 grams per cubic centimeter; the gaseous ones less than 2 grams per cubic centimeter.

PLANETARY NEBULA A compact ring or oval nebula that is made of material thrown out of a hot star.

The term "planetary nebula" is a misnomer; dying stars create these cocoons when they lose outer layers of gas. The process has nothing to do with planet formation, which is predicted to happen early in a star's life.

The term originates from a time when people, looking through weak telescopes, thought that the nebulae resembled planets within the solar system, when in fact they were expanding shells of glowing gas in far-off galaxies.

PLANETESIMAL Small rocky bodies one kilometer to hundreds of kilometers across.

The word especially relates to materials that exist in the early stages of the formation of a star and its planets from the dust of a nebula, which will eventually group together to form planets. Some are rock, others a mixture of rock and ice.

PLANKTON Microscopic creatures that float in water.

PLASMA A collection of charged particles that behaves something like a gas. It can conduct an electric charge and be affected by magnetic fields.

PLASTIC The ability of certain solid substances to be molded or deformed to a new shape under pressure without cracking.

PLATE A very large unbroken part of the crust of a planet. Also called tectonic plate.

On Earth the tectonic plates are dragged across the surface by convection currents in the underlying mantle.

PLATEAU An upland plain or tableland.

PLUTO The ninth planet from the Sun and six planets farther from the Sun than the Earth.

Pluto is one of the rocky planets, but it is very different from the others, perhaps being a mixture of rock and ice. It is about two-thirds the size of our Moon.

POLE The geographic pole is the place where a line drawn along the axis of rotation exits from a body's surface.

Magnetic poles do not always correspond with geographic poles.

POLYMER A compound that is made up of long chains formed by combining molecules called monomers as repeating units. ("Poly" means many, "mer" means part.)

PRESSURE The force per unit area.

PROBE An unmanned spacecraft designed to explore our solar system and beyond.

Voyager, Cassini, and Magellan are examples of probes.

PROJECTILE An object propelled through the air or space by an external force or an on-board engine.

PROMINENCE A cloud of burning ionized gas that rises through the Sun's chromosphere into the corona. It can take the form of a sheet or a loop.

PROPELLANT A gas, liquid, or solid that can be expelled rapidly from the end of an object in order to give it motion.

Liquefied gases and solids are used as rocket propellants.

PROPULSION SYSTEM The motors or rockets and their tanks designed to give a launcher or space vehicle the thrust it needs.

PROTEIN Molecules in living things that are vital for building tissues.

PROTONS Positively charged particles from the core of an atom.

PROTOSTAR A cloud of gas and dust that begins to swirl around; the resulting gravity gives birth to a star.

PULSAR A neutron star that is spinning around, releasing electromagnetic radiation, including radio waves.

QUANTUM THEORY A concept of how energy can be divided into tiny pieces called quanta, which is the key to how the smallest particles work and how they build together to make the universe around us.

QUASAR A rare starlike object of enormous brightness that gives out radio waves, which are thought to be released as material is sucked toward a black hole.

RADAR Short for radio detecting and ranging. A system of bouncing radio waves from objects in order to map their surfaces and find out how far away they are.

Radar is useful in conditions where visible light cannot be used.

RADIATION/RADIATE The transfer of energy in the form of waves (such as light and heat) or particles (such as from radioactive decay of a material).

RADIOACTIVE/RADIOACTIVITY The property of some materials that emit radiation or energetic particles from the nucleus of their atoms.

RADIOACTIVE DECAY The change that takes place inside radioactive materials and causes them to give out progressively less radiation over time.

RADIO GALAXY A galaxy that gives out radio waves of enormous power.

RADIO INTERFERENCE Reduction in the radio communication effectiveness of the ionosphere caused by sunspots and other increases in the solar wind.

RADIO TELESCOPE A telescope that is designed to detect radio waves rather than light waves.

RADIO WAVES A form of electromagnetic radiation, like light and heat. Radio waves have a longer wavelength than light waves.

RADIUS (pl. **RADII**) The distance from the center to the outside of a circle or sphere.

RAY A line across the surface of a planet or moon made by material from a crater being flung across the surface.

REACTION An opposition to a force.

REACTIVE The ability of a chemical substance to combine readily with other substances. Oxygen is an example of a reactive substance.

RED GIANT A cool, large, bright star at least 25 times the diameter of our Sun.

REFLECT/REFLECTION/REFLECTIVE To bounce back any light that falls on a surface.

REGULAR SATELLITES Satellites that orbit in the same direction as their parent planet. This motion is also called synchronous rotation.

RESOLVING POWER The ability of an optical telescope to form an image of a distant object.

RETROGRADE DIRECTION An orbit the opposite of normal—that is, a planet that spins so the Sun rises in the west and sinks in the east.

RETROROCKET A rocket that fires against the direction of travel in order to slow down a space vehicle.

RIDGE A narrow crest of an upland area.

RIFT A trench made by the sinking of a part of the crust between parallel faults.

RIFT VALLEY A long trench in the surface of a planet produced by the collapse of the crust in a narrow zone.

ROCKET Any kind of device that uses the principle of jet propulsion, that is, the rapid release of gases designed to propel an object rapidly.

The word is also applied loosely to fireworks and spacecraft launch vehicles.

ROCKET ENGINE A propulsion system that burns liquid fuel such as liquid hydrogen.

ROCKET MOTOR A propulsion system that burns solid fuel such as hydrazine.

ROCKETRY Experimentation with rockets.

ROTATION Spinning around an axis.

SAND DUNE An aerodynamically shaped hump of sand.

SAROS CYCLE The interval of 18 years $11^{1}/_{3}$ days needed for the Earth, Sun, and Moon to come back into the same relative positions. It controls the pattern of eclipses.

SATELLITE (1) An object that is in an orbit around another object, usually a planet.

The Moon is a satellite of the Earth.

See also: **IRREGULAR SATELLITE, MOON, GALILEAN SATELLITE, REGULAR SATELLITE, SHEPHERD SATELLITE.**

(2) A man-made object that orbits the Earth. Usually used as a term for an unmanned spacecraft whose job is to acquire or transfer data to and from the ground.

SATURN The sixth planet from the Sun and three planets farther away from the Sun than the Earth.

It is the least-dense planet in the solar system, having 95 times the mass of the Earth, but 766 times the volume. It is one of the gas giant planets.

SCARP The steep slope of a sharp-crested ridge.

SEASONS The characteristic cycle of events in the heating of the Earth that causes related changes in weather patterns.

SEDIMENT Any particles of material that settle out, usually in layers, from a moving fluid such as air or water.

SEDIMENTARY Rocks deposited in layers.

SEISMIC Shaking, relating to earthquakes.

SENSOR A device used to detect something. Your eyes, ears, and nose are all sensors. Satellites use sensors that mainly detect changes in radio and other waves, including sunlight.

SHEPHERD SATELLITES Larger natural satellites that have an influence on small debris in nearby rings because of their gravity.

SHIELD VOLCANO A volcanic cone that is broad and gently sloping.

SIDEREAL MONTH The average time that the Moon takes to return to the same position against the background of stars.

SILT Particles with a range of 2 microns to 60 microns across.

SLINGSHOT TRAJECTORY A path chosen to use the attractive force of gravity to increase the speed of a spacecraft.

The craft is flown toward the planet or star, and it speeds up under the gravitational force. At the correct moment the path is taken to send the spacecraft into orbit and, when pointing in the right direction, to turn it from orbit, with its increased velocity, toward the final destination.

SOLAR Anything to do with the Sun.

SOLAR CELL A photoelectric device that converts the energy from the Sun (solar radiation) into electrical energy.

SOLAR FLARE Any sudden explosion from the surface of the Sun that sends ultraviolet radiation into the chromosphere. It also sends out some particles that reach Earth and disrupt radio communications.

SOLAR PANELS Large flat surfaces covered with thousands of small photoelectric devices that convert solar radiation into electricity.

SOLAR RADIATION The light and heat energy sent into space from the Sun.

Visible light and heat are just two of the many forms of energy sent by the Sun to the Earth.

SOLAR SYSTEM The Sun and the bodies orbiting around it.

The solar system contains nine major planets, at least 60 moons (large natural satellites), and a vast number of asteroids and comets, together with the gases within the system.

SOLAR WIND The flow of tiny charged particles (called plasma) outward from the Sun.

The solar wind stretches out across the solar system.

SONIC BOOM The noise created when an object moves faster than the speed of sound.

SPACE Everything beyond the Earth's atmosphere.

The word "space" is used rather generally. It can be divided up into inner space—the solar system, and outer space—everything beyond the solar system, for example, interstellar space.

SPACECRAFT Anything capable of moving beyond the Earth's atmosphere. Spacecraft can be manned or unmanned. Unmanned spacecraft are often referred to as space probes if they are exploring new areas.

SPACE RACE The period from the 1950s to the 1970s when the United States and the Soviet Union competed to be first in achievements in space.

SPACE SHUTTLE NASA's reusable space vehicle that is launched like a rocket but returns like a glider.

SPACE STATION A large man-made satellite used as a base for operations in space.

SPEED OF LIGHT *See:* LIGHT-YEAR.

SPHERE A ball-shaped object.

SPICULES Jets of relatively cool gas that move upward through the chromosphere into the corona.

SPIRAL GALAXY A galaxy that has a core of stars at the center of long curved arms made of even more stars arranged in a spiral shape.

SPRING TIDE A tide showing the greatest difference between high and low tides.

STAR A large ball of gases that radiates light. The star nearest the Earth is the Sun.

There are enormous numbers of stars in the universe, but few can be seen with the naked eye. Stars may occur singly, as our Sun, or in groups, of which pairs are most common.

STAR CLUSTER A group of gravitationally connected stars.

STELLAR WIND The flow of tiny charged particles (called plasma) outward from a star.

In our solar system the stellar wind is the same as the solar wind.

STRATOSPHERE The region immediately above the troposphere where the temperature increases with height, and the air is always stable.

It acts like an invisible lid, keeping the clouds in the troposphere.

SUBDUCTION ZONES Long, relatively thin, but very deep regions of the crust where one plate moves down and under, or subducts, another. They are the source of mountain ranges.

SUN The star that the planets of the solar system revolve around.

The Sun is 150 million km from the Earth and provides energy (in the form of light and heat) to our planet. Its density of 1.4 grams per cubic centimeter is similar to that of a gas giant planet.

SUNSPOT A spiral of gas found on the Sun that is moving slowly upward, and that is cooler than the surrounding gas and so looks darker.

SUPERNOVA A violently exploding star that becomes millions or even billions of times brighter than when it was younger and stable.

See also: NOVA.

SYNCHRONOUS Taking place at the same time.

SYNCHRONOUS ORBIT An orbit in which a satellite (such as a moon) moves around a planet in the same time that it takes for the planet to make one rotation on its axis.

SYNCHRONOUS ROTATION When two bodies make a complete rotation on their axes in the same time.

As a result, each body always has the same side facing the other. The Moon and Venus are in synchronous rotation with the Earth.

SYNODIC MONTH The complete cycle of phases of the Moon as seen from Earth. It is 29.531 solar days (29 days, 12 hours, 44 minutes, 3 seconds).

SYNODIC PERIOD The time needed for an object within the solar system, such as a planet, to return to the same place relative to the Sun as seen from the Earth.

TANGENT A direction at right angles to a line radiating from a circle or sphere.

If you make a wheel spin, for example, by repeatedly giving it a glancing blow with your hand, the glancing blow is moving along a tangent.

TELECOMMUNICATIONS Sending messages by means of telemetry, using signals made into waves such as radio waves.

THEORY OF RELATIVITY A theory based on how physical laws change when an observer is moving. Its most famous equation says that at the speed of light, energy is related to mass and the speed of light.

THERMOSPHERE A region of the upper atmosphere above the mesosphere.

It absorbs ultraviolet radiation and is where the ionosphere has most effect.

THRUST A very strong and continued pressure.

THRUSTER A term for a small rocket engine.

TIDE Any kind of regular, or cyclic, change that occurs due to the effect of the gravity of one body on another.

We are used to the ocean waters of the Earth being affected by the gravitational pull of the Moon, but tides also cause a small alteration of the shape of a body. This is important in determining the shape of many moons and may even be a source of heating in some.

See also: NEAP TIDE and SPRING TIDE.

TOPOGRAPHY The shape of the land surface in terms of height.

TOTAL ECLIPSE When one body (such as the Moon or Earth) completely obscures the light source from another body (such as the Earth or Moon).

A total eclipse of the Sun occurs when it is completely blocked out by the Moon.

A total eclipse of the Moon occurs when it passes into the Earth's shadow to such a degree that light from the Sun is completely blocked out.

TRAJECTORY The curved path followed by a projectile.

See also: SLINGSHOT TRAJECTORY.

TRANSPONDER Wireless receiver and transmitter.

TROPOSPHERE The lowest region of the atmosphere, where all of the Earth's clouds form.

TRUSS Tubing arrayed in the form of triangles and designed to make a strong frame.

ULTRAVIOLET A form of radiation that is just beyond the violet end of the visible spectrum and so is called "ultra" (more than) violet. At the other end of the visible spectrum is "infra" (less than) red.

UMBRA (1) A region that is in complete darkness during an eclipse.

(2) The darkest region in the center of a sunspot.

UNIVERSE The entirety of everything there is; the cosmos.

Many space scientists prefer to use the term "cosmos," referring to the entirety of energy and matter.

UNSTABLE In atmospheric terms the potential churning of the air in the atmosphere as a result of air being heated from below. There is a chance of the warmed, less-dense air rising through the overlying colder, more-dense air.

UPLINK A communication from Earth to a spacecraft.

URANUS The seventh planet from the Sun and four planets farther from the Sun than the Earth.

Its diameter is four times that of the Earth. It is one of the gas giant planets.

VACUUM A space that is entirely empty. A vacuum lacks any matter.

VALLEY A natural long depression in the landscape.

VELOCITY A more precise word to describe how something is moving, because movement has both a magnitude (speed) and a direction.

VENT The tube or fissure that allows volcanic materials to reach the surface of a planet.

VENUS The second planet from the Sun and our closest neighbor.

It appears as an evening and morning "star" in the sky. Venus is very similar to the Earth in size and mass.

VOLCANO A mound or mountain that is formed from ash or lava.

VOYAGER A pair of U.S. space probes designed to provide detailed information about the outer regions of the solar system.

Voyager 1 was launched on September 5, 1977. Voyager 2 was launched on August 20, 1977, but traveled more slowly than Voyager 1. Both Voyagers are expected to remain operational until 2020, by which time they will be well outside the solar system.

WATER CYCLE The continuous cycling of water, as vapor, liquid, and solid, between the oceans, the atmosphere, and the land.

WATER VAPOR The gaseous form of water. Also sometimes referred to as moisture.

WEATHERING The breaking down of a rock, perhaps by water, ice, or repeated heating and cooling.

WHITE DWARF Any star originally of low mass that has reached the end of its life.

X-RAY An invisible form of radiation that has extremely short wavelengths just beyond the ultraviolet.

X-rays can go through many materials that light will not.

SET INDEX

Using the set index

This index covers all eight volumes in the *Space Science* set:

Vol. no. Title
1: *How the universe works*
2: *Sun and solar system*
3: *Earth and Moon*
4: *Rocky planets*
5: *Gas giants*
6: *Journey into space*
7: *Shuttle to Space Station*
8: *What satellites see*

An example entry:
Index entries are listed alphabetically.

——————/——————
Moon rover **3:** 48–49, **6:** 51
——————————/

Volume numbers are in bold and are followed by page references.

In the example above, "Moon rover" appears in Volume 3: *Earth and Moon* on pages 48–49 and in Volume 6: *Journey into space* on page 51. Many terms are also covered separately in the Glossary on pages 58–64.

See, see also, or *see under* refers to another entry where there will be additional relevant information.